100
answers to
100 questions

ve smart

---

about
loving
your Wife

100 answers to 100 questions about loving your wife

Christian LIFE

A STRANG COMPANY

Most CHRISTIAN LIFE products are available at special quantity discounts for bulk purchase for sales promotions, premiums, fund-raising, and educational needs. For details, write Christian Life, 600 Rinehart Road, Lake Mary, Florida 32746, or telephone (407) 333-0600.

100 Answers to 100 Questions About Loving Your Wife

Published by Christian Life
A Strang Company
600 Rinehart Road
Lake Mary, Florida 32746

www.strang.com

Scripture quotations marked CEV are from the Contemporary English Version, copyright © 1995 by the American Bible Society. Used by permission.

Scripture quotations marked THE MESSAGE are from *The Message: The Bible in Contemporary English*, copyright © 1993, 1994, 1995, 1996, 2000, 2001, 2002. Used by permission of NavPress Publishing Group.

Scripture quotations marked NIV are from the Holy Bible, New International Version. Copyright © 1973, 1978, 1984, by International Bible Society. Used by permission.

Scripture quotations marked NLT are from the Holy Bible, New Living Translation, copyright © 1996, 2004. Used by permission of Tyndale House Publishers, Inc., Wheaton, IL 60189. All rights reserved.

Scripture quotations marked NRSV are from the New Revised Standard Version of the Bible. Copyright © 1989 by the Division of Christian Education of the National Council of the Churches of Christ in the USA. Used by permission.

Cover design by Whisner Design Group, Tulsa, Oklahoma

ISBN 10: 1-59979-277-X
ISBN 13: 978-1-59979-277-4

BISAC Category: Religion/Christian Life/Love & Marriage

First Edition

08 09 10 11 12—9 8 7 6 5 4 3 2 1

Printed in the United States of America

Happy marriages begin when
we marry the ones we love,
and they blossom when we
love the ones we marry.

Tom Mullen

C o n t e n t s

Loving Your Wife by Supporting Her

Loving Your Wife by Protecting Her

Loving Your Wife by Helping Her Love Herself

Loving What's Different About Your Wife

Introduction

You had the girl and the ring, so you figured marriage, of course, was the next step. And what a big step it turned out to be, one that took you into uncharted territory. You thought you were prepared to be a loving husband, but after crossing that threshold you quickly realized that you had much to learn about loving your wife. And you may have been surprised to discover how long the learning process is. All those jokes about men not being able to understand women? Those aren't jokes—they are statements of fact. Your wife is a fascinating mystery, and you need to get a clue.

You want to be all your wife wants in a husband. You want to love her in a way that lives up to her expectations. And you will, as soon as you can find answers to all those questions you have on how to love her. *Love* is turning out to be a much bigger word than you previously thought, and it encompasses so much. Where does a man start when he wants to improve as a husband? With a question, and as a husband your first question must be, "How can I really, truly love my wife?"

That question opens the floodgates as many more questions come to mind. You will start with a hundred questions, and as the years unfold you will probably have at least another hundred. But you will be discovering the answers all along. Be a lifetime learner. Your wife will love you for it.

> As the Scriptures say, "A man leaves his father and mother and is joined to his wife, and the two are united into one." This is a great mystery, but it is an illustration of the way Christ and the church are one. So again I say, each man must love his wife as he loves himself.
>
> Ephesians 5:31–33, NLT
>
> The fulfillment of marriage is that joy in which each lover's true being is flowering because its growth is being welcomed and unconsciously encouraged by the other in the infinite series of daily decisions which is their life together.
>
> J. Neville Ward

1   question

What does your wife long to hear from you?

You said, "I love you," when you proposed. You probably still say it on your wedding anniversary and her birthday, and you write it in Valentine cards. And that says it all, right? What more could she possibly want? She has your heart, your constancy, and your paycheck. Doesn't that say it all? No, actually, it doesn't. So, you wonder, what is your wife hoping to hear from you when she looks at you with anticipation in her smile?

answer

Your wife longs to hear you say she's pretty. Today's woman enjoys success on many fronts, but no matter how successful she is, no matter how many friends she has, no matter what else is good in her life, she still needs to know that you find her attractive. In a society that highly prizes beauty, she can start feeling a little insecure about her femininity as her figure shifts during those childbearing years or when little lines start showing on her face. She wants to know that you find her attractive in spite of her postpartum tummy, and that you prize those laugh lines around her face as proof of a beautiful spirit. She wants to know you can still find something beautiful in a body that fought cancer and won. She wants to be reassured that, in spite of her imperfections, you still adore and desire her. She wants to hear you say, "You're still beautiful to me."

That new hairstyle she got? She did it so you would notice her. That time she spends in front of the mirror? It's for you. When she asks if the pants she's wearing make her look fat, she's really asking if you still think she looks like hot stuff. She wants to be reassured. She wants to feel confident. And the person who can do that for her is you. If you want your wife to shine and be happy, tell her she's pretty.

worth thinking about

- ▶ **Women fall in love** through what they hear. The kind things you say go right to your wife's heart. So when she comes downstairs ready for an evening out, make sure you tell her how nice she looks.

- ▶ **Notice when your wife** has a new dress or a new hairstyle and compliment her. She really did it for you, and it will mean a lot when you admire her efforts.

- ▶ **Accentuate the positive.** Even when your wife doesn't look her best, you can probably still find something to compliment. And if you do, you'll help her feel good about herself.

> *How beautiful you are, my darling!*
> *Oh, how beautiful!*
> Song of Songs 1:15, NIV

2 question

What should be the three most important words in your vocabulary?

Learning vocabulary was an important part of your education back when you were a kid in school. As a married man, you find that vocabulary is important once more as you go for that master's degree in the language of love. Everything you say to your wife is important, but three words in particular are the cement that makes your marriage's foundation firm. What are those key words you need to know to be a good husband?

answer

You may have already guessed. The words *I love you* are the three top vocabulary words you need to know. With those words you can enjoy close times and get through hard times. They are the words you want to tell your wife on a regular basis.

Everyone needs to feel loved, and for a woman, part of feeling loved is hearing often that she is. Every time you tell your wife you love her, you prove that she's important to you. Every time you say those vital words, you reassure her that you still want to be with her. Those three little words say, "I value you and would marry you again in a heartbeat." Those three little words say, "I don't care that you're not perfect. I still prefer you above all others." They tell her that she can rest easy regarding the future because no matter what, you'll be there to face it with her. The words *I love you* tell her she's desirable, assure her that she's valuable, and reaffirm that you're hers and that she won't need to ever doubt your faithfulness. Those three words are hard to overuse, so don't just pull them out during momentous occasions. By all means say them when you've had a fight and are making up, but also sprinkle them into your everyday married life. When you do this, you will season your married life with happiness.

worth thinking about

▶ Choose unexpected moments to tell her you love her—perhaps when you're enjoying a sunset together or getting ready to cuddle up on the couch and watch a movie. Surprise declarations of love are always a treat.

▶ Be sure you tell her you love her when she has done something to upset you. She will appreciate it.

▶ When you are apart, end every day with "I love you." Those three words will keep you close no matter how much physical distance separates you.

> *There is no stronger tie upon a woman than the knowledge that she is loved.*
> Madame de Motteville

3

When's the best time to tell her you love her?

You may have noticed that your wife seems more receptive to your declaration of love at some times than she does at others. Sometimes you tell her what she wants to hear, and instead of getting the reaction you expect, you are met with a lukewarm response or a cocked eyebrow. This can leave a man scratching his head, muttering, "I don't get it. I thought she wanted to hear that I love her. What am I doing wrong?"

answer

This is a timing issue and easily fixed. Women are not always as straightforward as men. They read body language and look for nuances. They check behind words for motivation. So the best time to tell your wife you love her is any time there is nothing in it for you. Of course she wants to hear that you love her when you're being intimate. But if the only time she hears it is when you're hoping to be physically intimate, she will soon find those words cheap. She'll figure that you tell her this only because you want something.

It's also not good timing to make a habit of telling her you love her right before you surprise her with unpleasant news or ask something of her you know she won't be thrilled to give. Her ulterior-motive detector will quickly spot that for sneaky manipulation. And if she's mad at you, a desperate "I love you" won't necessarily get you out of the doghouse.

The times she will most appreciate hearing those words are when you sneak up on her with them and surprise her. Tell her you love her when there is absolutely no chance she can suspect you of an ulterior motive. True affection means everything to her, and she'll cherish those simple unexpected declarations of love because she'll know the words sprang from an overflowing heart and from feelings of friendship and companionship.

worth thinking about

▶ Plan some times when you can pull out a surprise "I love you"—maybe when she's cooking dinner or when you're both in the car. Back it up with mentioning something you appreciate about her and how she enriches your life.

▶ Tell her you love her after you've been intimate, and be sure to include plenty of cuddling.

▶ Try to begin and end the day with these words. It will start your day off on the right foot and end it on a positive note. It will also serve as a reminder during tough times why you're together.

> *Affection is responsible for nine-tenths of whatever solid and durable happiness there is in our lives.*
> C. S. Lewis

4

question

How can you resolve conflict without creating a bigger problem?

As much as you love each other, you don't always see eye to eye, and sometimes that difference in vision can escalate to disagreement. You understand differences of opinion and arguments are inevitable, but you don't want those arguments filled with harsh words that end in tears. You want to find a way to settle differences that doesn't leave you feeling frustrated or her feeling hurt. How can a husband handle conflict in a loving way?

answer

Your wife feels things deeply on an emotional level. Those emotions are good because they equip her to be the heart and soul of your family. Without her strong emotional drive, birthdays and holidays wouldn't be half so special, and your house would lack much of the warmth that makes it feel like home.

Because she is primarily motivated by feelings, she tends to think you are, too. So when you clash over something, it can be hard for her to not take your statements personally. When you say something like "I don't want to spend money on a new car right now," you may be thinking, *I don't want to fork out money that's not in the budget.* But when she hears those words, she may interpret them as, *He doesn't care that I'm driving the kids around in this beater that could break down any minute.* Although you're discussing the budget, she is hearing your words in the language of emotion, and in that language you're saying, "I don't care about you." When you disagree, it's important to stop and remember that you are a team. Remind her that you love her and that it's not your intention to make her miserable. Make sure she is really hearing what you are saying. By doing so you give the two of you a plumb line to resolve conflict in a way that will help keep tempers from flaring and feelings from getting hurt.

worth thinking about

▶ **When you've got** a big issue to deal with, take a moment before discussing it to pray together and ask God to give both of you wisdom. Hold hands when you do this to remind yourselves of the unity you have as a couple.

▶ **When you disagree,** avoid using powder-keg word combinations like "I'm sick of" or "Why can't you understand?" These don't inspire unity because they imply she's the problem.

▶ **Deliver your arguments** without a raised voice. That signals anger, and anger triggers defensiveness. Remember, you want to work together to solve your problem.

> *Never let a problem to be solved become more important than a person to be loved.*
> Barbara Johnson

5 question

In what little ways can you say "I love you"?

You're both watching a movie where the hero says something cleverly romantic, and as your wife sighs longingly, you think, *Thanks a lot, guy. How do I compete with that?* For most men, the thought of pulling off the kind of verbal wooing that comes so easily to poets and Hollywood scriptwriters is intimidating. You love your wife dearly and would do anything for her. But putting what's in your heart into words is a challenge. What can a husband do?

answer

Tell your wife how much she means to you with small, creative strokes. When it comes to love, women are into details. And words are one of the most important details for any woman. Words mean a lot. That's why your wife puts a good deal of thought into picking out greeting cards for people she cares about. The message inside those cards is hugely important to her, and she'll spend a lot of time choosing the right one for each occasion. And when someone does the same for her, she feels loved and happy. She'll even keep cards or thank-you notes from her friends so she can relive the happy buzz again and again. For her, receiving fun little messages and love notes is the equivalent of a successful treasure hunt. Those reaffirming messages are treasures for her heart, and getting something special from you is like finding diamonds.

The most valuable gems are the ones you give your wife when no special occasion demands it. You don't have to write a long message, and it doesn't have to be poetry worthy of Robert Browning. Just a quick thought to let her know you think she's special will do the trick. And don't be surprised if she tucks your note away somewhere in a fancy little box or cute container. That note might not have cost you much, but to her, it will always be valuable.

worth thinking about

▶ **Slip a love note** into her purse before you both leave for work. It won't take you more than a couple of minutes, but the good feelings you inspire in her will last all day long.

▶ **Sign more** than just your name on her birthday card or gift tag. Tell her how she makes your life great. Doing this automatically doubles the value of your gift.

▶ **When you're stuck** for inspiration, think in terms of catchy words you see on Valentine heart candies: *be mine, hot stuff, kiss me, luv you.* You can say a lot with a little.

> *Kind words do not cost much,*
> *but they accomplish much.*
> Blaise Pascal

Why are words important?

A man finds joy in giving an apt reply—and how good is a timely word!

Proverbs 15:23, NIV

6

question

▼

What words are best left unspoken?

You want to continue to enjoy an open relationship with your wife, where you can always feel free to say what you think. But you are beginning to notice that there are some thoughts she prefers you to keep to yourself. If you answer a question honestly or make an observation, you can land in the doghouse. Obviously, there are some things that a man shouldn't say no matter how true they are, no matter what he thinks. For future reference, what are they?

answer

▼

Some words and their variations are hot buttons for a woman. The word *fat* probably tops the list. And there is no acceptable synonym for it, either. *Chunky, pudgy, big*— these words are just as depressing, and if you use them in reference to her, she'll still know what you're saying. It may not bother you that she's pudgy, but it probably bothers her, so don't let anyone trick you into using it to describe her. And any helpful comments to remind her of her condition won't encourage her to pass up that ice cream. They'll just make her feel discouraged or angry, and chances are that instead of being inspired to abstain, she'll dive face-first into the carton.

The word *dumb* insults her intelligence and is not a wise choice, either. Even using such a word obliquely will have the same effect. Don't say, "Well, babe, that was dumb," and expect her to shrug off your remark with a chuckle. There are times to be honest, but when your wife is still smarting from having made an error in judgment or an embarrassing mistake, that time isn't one of them.

To you, these may simply be honest remarks and no big deal, but they rattle her self-esteem and make her worry that her approval rating as a wife has slipped. Always remember before you speak, perception—her perception—is everything. Of course, still be yourself, but if you strive to always be the diplomatic version of yourself, your wife will thank you for it.

worth thinking about

▶ Keep unhelpful thoughts to yourself. The best way to deal with some faults is to overlook them and leave it to God to work on her.

▶ When tempted to make brutally honest observations, resist. If you see a need for change, talk in terms of *we* rather than *you*: "Maybe we should work on improving our eating habits."

▶ When she has messed up, don't use disparaging words to point out where she went wrong. Instead, give her emotional support before you begin assessing the damage. Always choose words that build up, and she'll have the confidence to overcome anything.

> *The mind of the wise makes his speech judicious.*
> Proverbs 16:23, NRSV

7 question

How should you teach your children to speak to their mother?

Smart-aleck kids. You see them everywhere: on sitcoms or commercials on TV, at the mall. But what about in your own house? Even though rude remarks seem to be normal childhood and adolescent behavior for modern-day America, how "normal" should you allow your children to be when they're talking to your wife? She is, after all, their mother and the woman you love. What is the right way for them to speak to her, and what role do you play in teaching it?

answer

One of the most important life tools for any child is the ability to treat others with respect. The safest place to learn this is at home, and you are the best teacher. You can help the learning process by insisting your children speak respectfully to their mother. As a father, you can lead both by instruction and by example. You can teach your children from a young age to speak politely to their mother by correcting them when they wander into disrespectful territory and test the occasional sitcom-style insult or when they forget to incorporate the words *please* and *thank you* into their vocabulary. Correcting a child when she raises her voice to her mother is also in order.

Everyone gets frustrated from time to time, even children, but speaking disrespectfully is not a useful tool for any child's toolbox, so don't let your child form this habit.

Children are incredible mimics. Yours will quickly learn to copy what they see you do. If you make jokes at your wife's expense, they soon will, too. If you speak ungraciously to her, so will they. On the other hand, if you treat your wife with the respect her position in the family deserves, your children are going to be more likely to do the same. Teaching them to speak respectfully to their mother is the first step toward teaching them to respect other authority figures. Your wife will thank you for your diligence in this, and, eventually, so will the rest of society.

worth thinking about

▶ Nip put-downs and rude retorts in the bud with swift justice. A simple "Don't talk to your mother like that" can effectively remind children of the respect due their mother. It will also demonstrate to them and her that you are behind her 100 percent.

▶ Ask politely when you need your wife's help. She'll appreciate the consideration, and the children will see firsthand how well manners and consideration work.

▶ Reinforce respectful behavior with a nod and a smile when your child speaks politely to his mother. A smile from a proud father is a powerful method of positive reinforcement.

> The greatest thing a father can do for his children is to love their mother.
> Josh McDowell

8

question

What's the one word you should never say?

You've already realized there are many things a husband shouldn't say, not if he wants to be happily married. But is there one key danger to avoid in your marriage, one word that should never, ever be uttered? Is there something a man can say that will send him down the slippery slope that leads to a broken marriage? What is the worst thing you can say, the explosive word that will set a fuse to your relationship and blow it up?

answer

The one word that should never be spoken between two people who have committed to each other is the word *divorce*. This word should never be uttered, no matter how hurt or angry you are, because it opens the door to that ugly option. You are a team, two people brought together to function as one unit. True love is tough. It rises above difficult circumstances and pushes on even when the loved one isn't being lovely. Divorce says, "There is nothing good here. There's no hope left. Cut the cord and get out. Start again." But Love says, "This is the one you chose. You found something to love once. Look again. Hang in there. Stay loyal."

The word *divorce* may enter your mind, but don't let it leave your mouth. Don't let it slip onto the negotiating table, either as a threat or an option, because once you have put it out there you've picked a deadly fruit. Eating it will not make your life better. Divorce doesn't end any marital problem because it doesn't address the root of your conflict. It doesn't teach you and your wife how to change or negotiate or look for the good in each other. It doesn't make you a better person or help you work on fixing the problem. It doesn't salve your hurts. All it does is create new problems. Concentrate instead on throwing out words that will heal and build, and both you and your marriage will benefit.

worth thinking about

▶ When things aren't going well, make a list of the good things about your wife and carry it in your wallet so you can look at it when you're feeling angry or frustrated.

▶ Look for external forces that might be bringing out the worst in both of you and see what you can do to change them for the better.

▶ Find an older and wiser head to talk to before you say something rash and set events in motion you'll regret later. Most problems can be worked out with time and patience.

> *A man leaves his father and mother and gets married. He becomes like one person with his wife. Then they are no longer two people, but one. And no one should separate a couple that God has joined together.*
>
> Mark 10:7–9, CEV

question

Why is it so important to say "I'm sorry"?

Your wife knows you'd never deliberately hurt her. Surely she knows you feel bad when she's not happy. It's so hard to say "I'm sorry." Do you really need to? Couldn't you just substitute a nice gesture, like bringing home flowers? Flowers say it all, right? Okay, maybe not. Why is learning to offer up these two words so important to keeping your wife's heart tender and your marriage healthy? What makes them so potent?

answer

Mastering the sincere use of these two words is the single most important thing you can do to keep your marriage healthy. And yet they are the hardest to say because no one speaks them without cost to his pride. They demand vulnerability. You may fear that if you say them to your wife you will open yourself up to attack or verbal retaliation like "You should be sorry." When you say you're sorry, you also risk a response that demands to know what you're going to do about it. And that could mean sacrifice or risk or simply irritation and inconvenience. To say "I'm sorry" is the equivalent of admitting you're wrong. And who likes to admit to his wife that he's wrong?

To say those words can feel like you're giving away all your power as a man. But saying "I'm sorry" also sends another message that goes beyond who's right and who's wrong. It says, "I choose you over my pride." These two words have the power to stop an argument dead in its tracks. They are the first step in healing hurt feelings. When you say them you are assuring your wife that you love her more than anything or anyone, including yourself. These words bring with them an underlying pledge that you won't be stubborn and selfish at the risk of your relationship. They proclaim that you'd rather be real than self-righteous. Use them generously, and you'll keep your marriage healthy.

worth thinking about

▶ Make sure you deliver your apology with love. Saying "I'm sorry" in an irritable or defensive voice rarely improves a bad situation.

▶ If you've hurt her publicly, make sure you tell her you're sorry publicly, too. Fair is fair.

▶ Say that you're sorry when you're right but she's upset. You don't need to apologize for what you think, but you can be sorry for how she feels. "I'm sorry that hurt you," coupled with a loving hug, makes a strong power tool for fixing any problem.

> It takes true courage to stand up in the face of those everyday indiscretions we all make and say, "I was wrong. I'm sorry."
> Staci Stallings

10

question

When is it good to talk about your wife?

You've heard that it's never good to talk about your wife. There's a reason for that advice. Like women, guys talk. They like to know who is in the doghouse and who is king of the bedroom. They like to commiserate with whoever's got the never-ending honey-do list and advise whoever appears to be henpecked. These conversations aren't helpful. But there are actually times when it's good to talk about your wife. What times are those, and what should you say?

answer

You absolutely should talk about your wife when you have an audience. Not to complain about her. That is gossip. Not to share intimate details that would embarrass her. That is crass. But by all means, brag about her. Feel free to share that she's the best cook in ten counties, or to express gratitude that she's putting you through law school. Feel free to defend her when your buddies suggest that she's to blame for the decreasing number of nights you go out with the boys. And especially feel free to talk about your wife right in front of her.

People like to hear good things said about them, and your wife is no exception. When you sing her praises to other people and she's there to hear it, you will make her day. Every wife gets a secret thrill when she and her husband are at a party and he just happens to mention in passing that she's fabulous. Or that she still looks great. Or that he couldn't imagine life with anyone else. Or that she's a great cook. The compliments don't have to be big or flowery, just heartfelt. When you say good things about your wife, you're not only being a good ambassador for marriage and encouraging her, but you are also strengthening the relationship by reminding yourself why you're committed to her. So go ahead and talk. It will do you both good.

worth thinking about

▶ **When your friends** are complaining about their wives, don't join in. Instead, find something positive to say about yours.

▶ **Train your ears** to pick up on wifely hints when you're together with friends. If she's talking about how busy she is, jump in and say how much you appreciate everything she does. If she's wondering if she spent too much on a dress, it's the perfect time to say, "But you look great in it." Little comments can buy big smiles.

▶ **Feel free** to say something good about your wife at a party without waiting for a hint. That's even better.

> *The right word at the right time is*
> *like precious gold set in silver.*
> Proverbs 25:11, CEV

question

When should you say no to your wife?

You love your wife and want to make her happy, so you don't like to say no to her about anything. But sometimes she comes up with ideas you can't get excited about. Sometimes she wants to purchase things you can't afford. Sometimes you simply can't get behind what she wants to do. When does a husband give up and give in, and when does he stand his ground and say, "No, I can't support that"?

answer

You should say no when you see trouble ahead. As a husband, it's up to you to "man up" and protect your wife and family, and sometimes the job description of family protector includes being the family wet blanket. Wet blankets tend to get a bad rap, but they aren't always bad. When there's a fire, they are a lifesaver.

If your wife takes your hand and tries to dance you toward the flames, don't be afraid to turn into a wet blanket. It's better to be wet and uncomfortable than burned. If she is dying to remodel the kitchen but wants to spend money that will stress the family budget, this is trouble on the horizon, and the only appropriate word is no. If your wife wants to go someplace with her girlfriends that you're concerned is inappropriate for a married woman, then your only appropriate vote is no, along with expressing the hope that she'd do the same for you if the situations were reversed. Yes, this is being a wet blanket. It is also protecting your relationship, which ultimately protects your wife and family. Today's world is peopled with empowered women, and it can be hard for a man to oppose his wife. But even though she may love her power, she still needs your protection. Don't be afraid to give it.

worth thinking about

▶ **Have a good explanation** as well as a good reason for saying no. Simply saying, "We can't afford that," isn't half as effective as taking time to review your budget together so she can see exactly why you "can't afford that."

▶ **The word** *no* can sometimes be coupled with other words like *Let's wait* or *Let's negotiate* or, even better, *Let's pray*.

▶ **It's okay to feel** strongly against something, but it's not okay to throw your power around. Always veto her suggestions gently.

> *Better, though difficult,*
> *the right way to go*
> *Than wrong, tho' easy,*
> *where the end is woe.*
> John Bunyan

12

question

If actions speak louder than words, what are you saying?

You tell your wife you love her all the time. Those words say a lot, but what you say isn't the only way you communicate to your wife how you feel about her. What you do sends an equally strong message. In fact, what you do gives her proof beyond a shadow of a doubt how much she means to you. How, exactly, do your actions either support or undermine those declarations of love?

answer

Words are a wonderful love currency, one that your wife values highly, but actions are the gold standard that backs them up. And when it comes to love, she is delighted when you become a man of action. Anyone can say "I love you," but doing "I love you," now that's a different story. Doing often involves unselfishness and sacrifice. Doing pulls a man away from the pregame show on TV. Doing can involve work, and it isn't always fun. And that is why it's so valuable—doing proves that you meant those words of love. The amount of time, money, energy, and emotional effort you spend on your marriage speaks volumes to your wife. When you say "I love you" and back it up with action, you give her proof positive that you mean what you say.

How much of you does your wife get when you're home? Does she have to pry the TV remote out of your hands? Does she have to beg for your cooperation in all things relating to the family, and, if so, how hard and how long? When was the last time you sacrificed something to help her with a project? Can she count on you to be there for her when she's got a problem? If someone were to ask your wife, "How do you know your husband loves you?" what would she answer? What would you want her to answer? Saying "I love you" is important. Living it is vital.

worth thinking about

▶ **Sit down** with your wife and ask her what your actions are saying about the way you feel about her. Find out what, to her, says love. Ask her to give you some specific tasks so you know exactly what to do.

▶ **Train yourself** to think in terms of her first. When making decisions about things pertaining to the house, instead of telling her what you'd like, find out what her preferences are.

▶ **When planning** leisure activities, think in terms of *we* instead of *me*.

> *Love is shown in your deeds,*
> *not in your words.*
> Father Jerome Cummings

13

▼

How can you show your wife she's special?

Your wife is one in a million. You knew it the moment you met her and got your game on to make sure you'd win her. Now she's yours, and when you look at her you realize you got the cream of the crop. She makes your day with her smile, and she makes your life with everything she does to make your house a home. You don't want her to think you take her for granted. How can you show her she's special?

answer

▼

The best way to show your wife she's special is to treat her accordingly. Remember your first car? You washed and waxed it regularly. You did all you could to guard it against dents and scratches. That car received a double dose of tender, loving care.

Of course a wife is not a car, but the same principle applies. The way you treat her will tell the world (and her) exactly what you think of her. So invest time and energy in loving her and give her the TLC treatment. Don't save grand gestures for anniversaries and birthdays. Occasionally import them into your everyday life.

Romantic treats and surprises will not only give her an emotional lift and take the humdrum out of her day, but they'll also boost her self-esteem. Showing her she's special doesn't have to be all about gifts and dinner out. You can let her know by using endearments when you talk to her. Don't be embarrassed to give her a cute nickname or refer to her as your love, your baby, or your best friend. She knows that special names are always a sign of close friendship and intimacy, and she'll be flattered by the honor. Honoring her when she least expects it will bring back those happy, romantic feelings you inspired in her when you were dating. And they'll reassure her that you haven't forgotten how special she is.

worth thinking about

▶ **Randomly select** one day every month to pick up flowers or some other small treat on the way home from work and surprise her.

▶ **Call her** from work once in a while just to tell her you love her or send her a text message listing the top three things you love about her.

▶ **Be generous** with your time. We spend the most time on what matters most to us. Show her she's special by giving her the time she deserves.

> *You can give without loving,*
> *but you cannot love without giving.*
> Amy Carmichael

question

How do your decisions reflect your love for your wife?

When you were single your decisions affected only you. And you could make decisions quickly and easily. Now that you're married, you realize that your decisions don't affect your life alone. They impact your wife as well. Add children to the mix, and now several people live with the consequences of what you decide. Keeping that in mind, how do your decisions reflect your love for your wife? What do you tell her with the choices you make?

answer

Decisions are the true measure of your love. They reveal your heart more than anything. To your wife, they say either "He loves me" or "He loves me not." When you make a decision to do something you know is going to make your mate unhappy, you tell her she doesn't matter. When you decide to spend money in a way that will impact her negatively or make commitments for which she will also pay, you announce, "I love myself better." This means if you buy that boat you always wanted and it puts a squeeze on the family finances, you have just proclaimed yourself captain of the SS *Selfish* and told your wife exactly where the family falls on your priority list. When you choose recreational activities that pull you away from family activities on a regular basis, you leave her wondering why you wanted to get married in the first place.

You telegraph a very different message when you make choices taking her feelings into consideration. Decisions made that way say, "I love you and am willing to sacrifice my wants so you can feel safe and happy." Whether you're considering a cross-country move, a major purchase, or an offer to join that slow-pitch team, you'll want to remember to add to your list of pros and cons the messages you'll be choosing to send along with the choice you make.

worth thinking about

▶ Before making any decision, ask yourself how your choice will affect your wife. Will it inconvenience her or require sacrifice? Is this something that she wants also?

▶ If you're not sure how she'll react to what you're considering, consult her. Find out how she feels before you commit yourself to anything that will involve or affect her.

▶ If you're considering something she's not excited about, ask if she can support you anyway. She wants you to be happy, and she'll be more inclined to be supportive if you let her be part of your decision-making process.

> *Husbands, love your wives, just as Christ loved the church and gave himself up for her.*
> Ephesians 5:25, NIV

15 question

What does home repair have to do with love?

Okay, so you have needed to fix that broken window screen since last August. Summer is half over, and it is still broken. You have been busy, but you will get to it eventually. Telling your wife that you have been busy won't always reassure her. There is no *eventually* in her vocabulary. Only *now*. And furthermore, in her mind there is a clear link between love and home repair. You're not sure you follow it. How can you connect the dots?

answer

Most women don't list home-repair skills on their home-making résumés. Home decor yes, but not home repairs. Chances are that your other half has no idea what a Phillips screwdriver is, or a shim or a plumb line. And she probably figures she doesn't need to learn about them anyway, not when she has you to be her "Tim the Tool Man," her go-to guy. She looks at a home-repair need and figures it won't take you long to fix the problem. So she asks you sweetly if you'll come to the rescue, assuming that you understand she wants this fixed ASAP. You agree, thinking you'll get to it when you get the chance.

And that is where the problem begins. You get busy with work, car maintenance, or the game on TV, and the honey-do project slips toward the bottom of your priority list. But she gets more irritated every time she looks at the project-in-waiting because she walks past it and thinks, *He's never going to get around to fixing this. He's not making time to do what I asked. He doesn't care.* Of course you care. And the best way to prove it is by shooting that home-repair need to the top of your priority list. If your buddy needed help with a project, you'd be right there. Remember that your wife is your number one buddy and do the good-neighbor thing first in your own home.

worth thinking about

▶ **Set aside** one day a month for home repairs. Having a regular appointment with your house will help you keep current on maintenance.

▶ **Communication is key.** Ask your wife to list her top priority projects, then make sure she understands what you can reasonably fix and when. Set goals and set dates to make them happen.

▶ **If a repair** is beyond you, admit it and hire someone qualified to do it. You'll get yourself off the hook, and your wife will be happy to see it get done.

> *Friends give generously to each other.*
> *Be generous in what you give your spouse.*
> Darrell L. Hines

What is the relationship between what you feel and what you do?

Love is not only something you feel. It is something you do.

David Wilkerson

question

▼

How can you prove you don't take your wife for granted?

When your wife accuses you of taking her for granted, it leaves you scratching your head. How can she say that when you do so much for her? You gave up the freedom of bachelorhood for her. Now you work long hours to give her a nice place to live and to support the family. She's the queen of your heart. You would never take her for granted. What kind of behavior proves what is in your heart?

answer

▼

Surprisingly, it doesn't take much to keep a wife from feeling taken for granted. How to avoid this problem can be summed up in one word: *consideration*. Consideration simply means thinking about how what you do or don't do will make her feel and then acting accordingly. You show consideration when you don't make assumptions. You show it when you don't assume her enthusiasm or cooperation in anything, but instead give her the opportunity to express her thoughts. You show it by checking her emotional temperature rather than making assumptions. Making assumptions makes her feel invisible, but checking with her before you commit to things tells her she's still an important part of the equation. So does occasionally changing your after-work routine. It's easy, comforting even, to fall into routines, but they can also make a relationship feel stale. Breaking them sometimes is a good way to show both of you that you don't take her for granted. Instead of ambling off to watch TV after dinner, once in a while ask her what she would like to do.

Showing appreciation is another important facet of consideration. If she's expended energy doing something special for you, a hug and a simple "Thank you" will assure her that you're paying attention. Acknowledge her presence and her importance in your life by treating her with the same consideration with which you want to be treated, and she won't worry that you take her for granted.

worth thinking about

▶ Instead of leaving dirty dishes and clothes in your wake, pick up after yourself. If you've left a mess and she's picked it up, thank her.

▶ Take time to let her know when you're running behind schedule and will be home late rather than assuming that she'll go with the flow, especially if it involves food preparation.

▶ Check with your wife before putting social engagements or volunteer commitments on your calendar. This sends a clear message to her that she's a top priority in your life.

> *Remember that women are ordinarily affectionate, passionate creatures, and as they love much themselves, so they expect much love from you.*
> Richard Baxter

question

▼

What small gestures earn you really big points?

You have heard it said that women value little things highly, but that's so vague. You need more specific suggestions. What little things? And do the same things work for all women? You know what says love to you, but what works for you doesn't necessarily work for your wife. So where do you start? Are there any one-size-fits-all gallantries that are guaranteed to score you big points and make you a champion husband?

answer

▼

This is not as hard as it looks. Any gesture that acknowledges her needs or desires and your willingness to meet them will fit the bill, especially when you do something that anticipates those needs and desires. When she comes home from grocery shopping and you meet her at the car, ready to help her pack in the family supplies, you're saying, "I know you're tired. Let me help."

Yes, there was a time when a man didn't dare open a door for a woman for fear she'd snarl, "I can do that myself." Those days are gone. This is the day of the princess. You see princess paraphernalia everywhere in the stores: cards, special tea towels, T-shirts, funny sayings to hang on the kitchen wall. Why are these so popular? They're popular because most women long to feel like a princess once in a while. The average woman spends most of her time working, cleaning, cooking, gardening, and chauffeuring kids to music lessons and sports activities. When a man opens a door for her, it makes her feel special. He anticipated a need and filled it before she even had to ask. Wow! That's princess living. When you open doors for your spouse, loosen the lid on that stubborn pickle jar, or carry something heavy for her, you are acknowledging and anticipating her need and putting your brawn at her service. This kind of small gesture won't cost you much in the way of time or energy, but the message behind it will earn you big points.

worth thinking about

▶ Step in and take on some gross household chore like emptying the garbage, and you'll be her modern-day Sir Walter Raleigh, throwing your cape over a muddy road so the lady doesn't have to get dirty.

▶ Another top-ten good-guy gesture is to remember to put down the toilet seat. She'll appreciate this hugely when she needs to use the bathroom in the middle of the night.

▶ If you're still mystified over what she'd appreciate, ask her to make a list to give you a jump start. She'll be happy to oblige.

> We husbands tend to believe love is demonstrated by our hard work, bringing home the paycheck, or in the vacations and other activities we plan on a grand scale. But our wives are looking for the little things.
>
> E. Glenn Wagner

18 question
▼
How do you show your love when you are out together?

Back when you were dating and under that exciting chemical and emotional concoction called "falling in love," you walked down the street holding on to each other as if you were sure you'd fall down if you let go. You smiled, you kissed, you kept your arm around her so other guys would know she was taken. You may not do that anymore, but you still tell the world exactly how you feel about your wife by the way you behave when you're out together.

answer
▼

Whether your marriage is new or comfortable and on autopilot, you still tell the world exactly how you feel about your wife by the way you speak to her and the way you interact with her. If you've fallen into a rut, think back to when you were first together. She wasn't your wife yet. She was just the hottest, smartest, sweetest, most interesting woman on the planet, the woman of your dreams, and the one you wanted to spend your life with. Simply seeing her made you smile.

Just because you can hug her any time at home doesn't mean you have to stop all contact when you're out together.

An arm around her shoulder proclaims you a united pair. When you're out as a couple and you put an arm around her waist, it announces to one and all (her included) that she is yours and that you value her. It also reassures her that you're there for her. When you smile at her from across a room, it telegraphs the message that you love her and still think she's special. Resist any temptation to make jokes at her expense. If she says something that you could easily take the wrong way, choose not to. Settle your arguments in private, and demonstrate your love in public. She is still the most important person in your life. When you behave like it in public, your private life will benefit, too.

worth thinking about

▶ **Take her hand** and give it a squeeze when you're walking into a party together or standing talking with other people. Never be embarrassed to kiss her hello or good-bye in front of someone.

▶ **Save your quarrels** for private times when you can honestly express your feelings and negotiate. Public quarrels not only embarrass her and make you look bad, but they also make the people around you uncomfortable.

▶ **Make a habit** of moving close and putting an arm around her shoulders when you're sitting together. Physical closeness is a comfort because it symbolizes emotional closeness.

> *I am my beloved's and my beloved is mine.*
> Song of Solomon 6:3, NRSV

question

How can you learn to work together as a team?

She's your favorite teammate, but sometimes working with your wife can be challenging. You may start a project with everything going smoothly and then halfway through, you wind up grinding your teeth or she winds up with steam coming out her ears. Moving a piece of furniture together or attempting a kitchen-sink repair operation can turn into a frustrating scene from a sitcom. How can you work together effectively?

answer

It's always a good idea to remember when working together with your wife on anything that you are teamed up with a person who is very different from you. Chances are, you'll each approach the same problem differently. Certainly your communication styles will be different, and that can lead to misunderstandings and hurt feelings. If you have to give her directions, your orders may come across as sharp rather than simply to the point. She may not understand what you want when you say, "Pass me that monkey wrench," or when you simply say, "Help me move this, will you?" Her response will probably be, "What? Where? How?" Keeping those differences in mind, be clear with your wife about what you need from her. If you talk her through the process of what you're going to do and let her ask questions until she understands what's required at her end, you'll save both of you a truckload of irritation.

Working together in love means communicating in love. It can be hard to be patient when you're wrestling under the sink with a leaky faucet, but try to avoid barking orders and speaking sharply. You know it's not her fault the faucet is leaking. Make sure she knows that by not snapping at her. Manners and consideration work wonders with your team on the job. They'll also work wonders with your teammate at home.

worth thinking about

▶ Add a "please" and "thank you" to your requests when working together. It will make her feel less like your flunky and more like your valued helper.

▶ Make sure you don't ask your wife to do things that are beyond her. She has muscles, but they're not as big as yours, and she may not be able to carry her end of the load. Literally. For those really tough jobs, recruit a guy.

▶ Whether you're setting up a budget or buying a house, begin any project you undertake together with prayer. This is the best groundwork you can lay.

> *Many marriages would be better if the husband and wife clearly understood they're on the same side.*
> Zig Ziglar

20

question

How can you meet both her needs and yours?

Maintaining a relationship takes time and effort, and your marriage is no exception. You want to meet your wife's needs, but spending time with her, helping her, and being there for her is a big job. This added on to the hours you spend working and commuting can leave you wondering how you can keep all those balls in the air, still be a good husband, and stake out any man time for yourself.

answer

Your wife needs to know you're there for her when she's got a problem or is upset, and of course she wants your company. But that doesn't translate into your being under house arrest every night. She doesn't require your presence 24-7. You can schedule in time for both her and the pursuit of worthwhile callings and interests. You can go to the gym or play some basketball to work off those tensions. You won't be doing your wife a service by ignoring every activity that defines who you are in order to be at her beck and call. You will be around that way, but you will be grumpy or boring, or both. To meet her needs, you must first be strong and emotionally and mentally fit yourself.

Yes, as a husband you often have to sacrifice. You can't do only the things you want to do and neglect her, but you can schedule activities into your life that will leave you refreshed and ready to be strong for her. She wants to know that you're there for her, but she also understands that your marriage isn't just about her, and she loves you enough to want you to be happy. So don't be the strong silent type. Make sure she understands what your needs are and how they help you be a better husband. She'll gladly help you meet them.

worth thinking about

▶ Organization is the key. Schedule in those trips to the gym you need so it becomes part of your family's overall activities calendar. Set aside time to develop a talent or pursue a hobby. Life can be planned around almost anything if it's on the calendar.

▶ Consult your wife when you're organizing to make sure your activities don't conflict with family commitments.

▶ Encourage her to take time for herself also. When you're both becoming all you can be individually, you'll be stronger as a couple.

> *There's an opportune time to do things, a right time for everything on the earth.*
> Ecclesiastes 3:1, The Message

21

question

When do your needs take a backseat to hers?

What about those times when you and your wife find yourselves in a situation where one person's needs aren't going to be met, where someone is going to have to sacrifice? You've looked at it from every angle, and you simply can't find a win-win solution. What do you do when an opportunity for you means a loss for her? When does a husband set aside his own needs to make sure his wife's needs are met?

answer

Put her needs first when her welfare is at stake. In an ideal situation, meeting your needs contributes to her welfare, and you can move forward as a couple, united. But not every situation is ideal. Different priorities, different visions, and different emotional and physical needs can make unity difficult to preserve. You may see a new job in another state as a great career opportunity, while she may perceive it as a loss of her family and support network. You may wish for more physical intimacy during a difficult pregnancy. She may not be able to accommodate you. Sometimes there is no compromise. There's either your way or her way. Those are the times when you can find yourselves stuck in a stalemate. No matter what you do, someone won't be happy. Still, love isn't always about happiness. Love is about loyalty and trust, so it's good to remember that a woman can have difficulty trusting a man who turns a deaf ear to her concerns and the cries of her heart. When you and your wife find yourselves in a situation where someone will suffer no matter what you decide, that is the time to put her needs above yours. That is when you transform yourself into a superhero and make superhuman sacrifices. Your goal as a husband is to love and protect your wife. You can do that when it comes down to a choice between your needs and her needs by putting hers first.

worth thinking about

▶ **When making big decisions** that affect both of you, discuss them, listing the pros and cons. That will give each of you the other's perspective. Seeing the positives, your wife may find she can support you. Or, seeing the negatives, you might not find it so hard to sacrifice for her.

▶ **When tempted** to feel resentful, remind yourself of how your unselfishness has strengthened your marriage.

▶ **Remember that life** is full of opportunity and change. You may be missing something now, but you could very well find consolation and reward farther down the road.

> *Getting what you want is not nearly as important as giving what you have.*
> Tom Krause

22

How do you learn your wife's hopes and dreams?

When you were first in love you shared your thoughts, hopes, and dreams with each other. Sometimes you stayed up all night talking. Now that you're married, you're sharing a life and building a home. Mostly you talk about bills, family needs, and home improvement. Hopes and dreams can easily get submerged under all that busyness. But they're still there. You want her to be all God made her to be. How do you learn what's hidden in her heart?

answer

One of the best ways to find her dreams is to look for them. This may involve some careful listening, as she may not share. And that can be for any number of reasons. Sometimes a woman gives up on her dreams because she decides she doesn't deserve them. She may reason, *I should have made different choices when I was younger. I didn't and now it's too late.* Women sometimes second-guess their husbands. A woman may easily assume her husband wouldn't support her pursuing something, and, rather than risk conflict, she'll simply bury the hope with a wistful "Oh, well." She may worry that to pursue her dream would be selfish. She may worry that if she fails she'll look foolish.

Your quest can be to find out where she buried those long-ago dreams and help her resurrect them. Find out how she'd love to use those gifts and talents. The best way to do that is simply to ask. Perhaps she has already told you. Now is the time to learn if that hope she once confided is still burning somewhere at the back of her mind. Maybe she never shared her dreams for the future. Maybe it looked like her biggest dream was to be with you. That one has come true. Does she have others? Does she have gifts and talents that she undervalues? You could point them out. Compliment and encourage her, and she'll feel safe to venture into new territory.

worth thinking about

▶ **Pay attention** to what sparks her enthusiasm. What section does she drift to in a bookstore? Does she watch a reality show about careers or house flipping and say, "I could do that"? There's a clue.

▶ **Listen to** what she says at parties or when she is talking on the phone to friends.

▶ **Take her away** from the distractions at home—out for dinner or for a walk—then ask questions that begin with phrases like "If you could do anything you wanted with your life . . ."

> *Give your dreams all you've got and you'll be amazed at the energy that comes out of you.*
> William James

question

How do you show your wife you are behind her 100 percent?

Your wife's talents and aspirations are all part of the unique package you fell in love with, and so of course you want her to succeed. You understand that, as a team, when one of you succeeds, both of you benefit. You want her to rest confidently in the knowledge that you are her biggest fan. How can you let her know that in all her endeavors, just as she's always there for you, you're there for her?

answer

Your support can come in many forms. In fact, it should. True support should be like a three-legged stool. The first leg of support is your words to her. How do you react when your wife comes to you with an idea for a home business? What do you say when she informs you that she's been asked to head the PTO fund-raiser? Are you negative or positive, encouraging or discouraging? You can appreciate her enthusiasm or her drive even if you're not sure about the way she's directing it. You can also applaud her unselfishness when she takes on volunteer tasks before voicing concern that she might not have the time to do them.

The second leg of support is your words to others. She knows you're on board when she hears you applaud her efforts to your family and friends rather than complain about the inconvenience to yourself.

And then there's that third leg of the stool: your actions. When you get behind your wife by what you do as well as by what you say, then you give her proof positive of your support. This may mean giving up time for yourself or pitching in and helping more at home. You may find yourself attending functions you'd rather pass on. Whatever form those actions take, do them, and you'll send the message loud and clear that you're there for her.

worth thinking about

▶ **You may not** always be on board with everything your wife wants to do. Look for alternate paths you can suggest to help her use her talents and realize her dream.

▶ **Make yourself** available for brainstorming. Offer your talents and time.

▶ **Make your support** visible. When she's in a play, be in the front row with flowers. Attend the fund-raiser she planned and spend some money for a good cause. Always be the first to applaud.

> *There are high spots in all of our lives and most of them have come about through encouragement from someone else. I don't care how great, how famous or successful a man or woman may be, each hungers for applause.*
> George Matthew Adams

question

How does being an involved dad support your wife?

You love your kids, and you are happy to support your family, to take them on vacation in the summer, to attend Little League games, and even to roll out of bed before the sun comes up on Christmas morning. Those are the marks of a good dad by your definition. Sometimes you suspect your wife wants more. But what? And how is it that she connects what you do with the kids to your relationship with her?

answer

Your wife understands that you have to work, but she also knows that both she and the children need your active, involved presence on a daily basis as much as they need your paycheck. She can do her best to pull your share of the parenting load as well as hers, but doing so will take a toll on her mentally, physically, and emotionally. She is not wired to interact with the children as both mother and father. She knows she can't offer a much-needed male viewpoint when your son asks her questions about guy things, and she certainly can't meet your daughter's need for daddy's attention. Trying to pick up the slack and give your children what time they crave with you can exhaust your wife and leave her feeling frustrated and resentful. A mother trying also to be a father feels as if she has been abandoned to carry a heavy load alone.

When your wife sees you interacting with your children on a regular basis, she feels supported. As you take an active interest in their lives, she is reassured that the two of you are a team. And she knows that because you are there for the children, you will be there for her, too. The two of you enriched your relationship when you brought children into the world. Now that they are here, you cement your relationship by working together to raise them well.

worth thinking about

▶ Go with your wife to parent-teacher conferences and open houses at school whenever possible. She wants your support and your input before, during, and after these important meetings.

▶ Be involved in the daily business of child rearing, and help with homework.

▶ Take a child to the park or with you when you run errands so that the child gets one-on-one time with Dad. You'll not only build a good relationship with your child, but you will also give your wife a break.

> *Children are a blessing and a gift from the* LORD.
> Psalm 127:3, CEV

25 question

How can you help your wife cope with failure?

Your wife loves to set goals and reach high, and you're proud of her for it. You're especially proud of her successes. But life isn't always about success. Even the most gifted person fails sometimes. You can cope with your own failures, but it's twice as hard to cope with hers. You feel helpless. What do you do when your wife fails? How do you ease the pain? How do you help her maintain a positive attitude and keep hope alive?

answer

Failure is a rude visitor. It often arrives unannounced, it's never pleasant, and it leaves its host feeling worthless and depressed. So if it visits your wife, be prepared to fight for her emotional welfare. Don't let a failure take away her hope.

You can do this by being quick to remind her that there is a big difference between failing and being a failure. Point out her successes and remind her of her talents. When things aren't going well is not the time for comments like "I told you that wouldn't work" or "You should have listened to me." Chances are you won't need to say anything because she'll say it for you. What she needs is the same thing you would if your positions were reversed: reassurance that you still believe in her. So tell her. And allow time for her to process her disappointment.

As you know, it takes time to heal emotional wounds. Don't expect her to suck it up and snap out of it. Instead, give her a listening ear and as much time and as many kind words as she needs to recover. There will come a time when she'll decide life is not as bleak as it looks, when she'll feel strong enough to try again. Until then, lend her your strength. Give her your support.

worth thinking about

▶ Give her hope for the future. Reassure her that other opportunities will come her way. Haul out old scrapbooks and remind her how much she's already accomplished.

▶ Accompany all pep talks with a hug. Your wife needs hugs when life is going good. Imagine how much more she needs them when it's not.

▶ When in doubt, ask what you can do to help her. There may be nothing you can do, but simply the fact that you asked will be a comfort.

> *Our focus must always be*
> *on building people up.*
> Dan Davis

Is it important to support and encourage your wife?

You must encourage one another each day.

Hebrews 3:13, CEV

26

What can you do when your wife is feeling frazzled?

Your wife is the heart of your family. Sometimes that heart can get to racing pretty fast. She often takes on more than she should, and when she does that there are times when emotional demands and the long to-do list can press in on her and put her in short-circuit mode. When this happens you know she needs help, but you're not always sure what kind of help. What can you, her husband, do when your wife reaches the point of pulling out her hair?

answer

It is easy for a woman to get frazzled when she feels like she's facing something overwhelming alone. So much to do, so many needs to meet, and there's only one of her. No one sees all she does; no one cares. When she starts feeling like that, her circuits begin to fry.

No matter what has got your wife frazzled, she will want emotional support. You can give it by seeing and acknowledging what she's going through, and appreciating it and then reassuring her that you've got her back. She may need to relieve her stress by expressing verbally how frustrated or overwhelmed she feels. Let her vent, because she needs you to listen. In the process of listening, you'll probably pick up clues as to what kind of help she wants.

Before you roll up your sleeves and jump in, first buoy her up with words of sympathy and praise. Verbal support can do a lot to repair frayed nerves. Once you've given her a shot of encouragement, step in and take over something on her to-do list. This will take a weight off her shoulders and give her a chance to regroup. And give her permission to take some time off. She'll never give it to herself, but if you insist, she'll get that R & R she needs. When she hears and sees that you're there for her, the frazzle factor will diminish.

worth thinking about

▶ **Sometimes it may** look to you like your wife is getting stressed about unimportant things, but try to keep that thought to yourself. If they are unimportant, she'll figure it out. Meanwhile, be sympathetic.

▶ **Be sure to add** touch to the equation. A hug or a quick shoulder rub can do a lot to reenergize a frazzled female.

▶ **Before pitching in** to help, ask for specific direction on what you can do to make her life less stressful. When in doubt, give her some chocolate.

> *There is no exercise better for the heart than reaching down and lifting people up.*
> John Andrew Holmes

27

What frustrates your wife, and how can you fix it?

Your wife does a great job of running your home, and she makes it a happy place to live. But there are times when she gets frustrated with the job and would just as soon go on strike. When she's frustrated, you're frustrated. Your desire as a husband is to enjoy a peaceful home with a happy wife. How can you make that happen? What's a key frustration that you can recognize and help alleviate?

answer

Frustrations can come in all shapes and sizes, but in the home one of the chief ones is often the children. Nothing is more wonderful or more precious than a child. And nothing can as effectively try a person's patience. Your wife takes her responsibilities as a mother seriously. Her goal is to raise great kids and provide the best home she can. You want this, too, but during much of the day you may be further removed from life in the domestic trenches. She is probably with the kids more than you, a lot more, which is where the frustration factor can come in. If your wife feels that she's reigning over chaos, if she finds herself wondering if she's simply talking to herself when she assigns tasks that get ignored, or if she sees her house rules being broken, she is going to get frustrated. Why is she trying so hard? No one is listening; no one is cooperating. You can save her much frustration by backing her up and reinforcing the rules. When you step in, it's like the cavalry riding to the rescue. It gives her a chance to breathe and reminds her that she's not manning the home front all by herself. Knowing she has your full support and cooperation alone won't make her life free of irritations, but it will certainly bring down the frustration level.

worth thinking about

▶ **Make a checklist** you can sign off on for completed chores and good behavior. Put a reward system in place to help motivate your children to cooperate with Mom.

▶ **Have regular** "board meetings" with your wife where you discuss and analyze how well family policies are working.

▶ **Make sure** you and your wife are in agreement on house rules and curfews. That way you'll avoid the frustration of having your authority undermined by a child trying to play one of you against the other.

> *Whoever heard of a child who is never disciplined by its father?*
> Hebrews 12:7, NLT

question

▼

How can you help
when she's trying
to lose weight?

Because you love your wife, you married her for richer
or poorer and promised to stick by her for better or for
worse and in sickness and in health, which you may
have noticed also means in thick or in thin. You're happy
with her no matter what, but you want to be supportive
when she's trying hard to get healthy and look good for
you. Dieting is not fun. How can you help?

answer

▼

Dieting seems to go hand in hand with being female.
Just as no man likes to lose his hair, no woman likes to
lose her waistline. Having a nice figure is important to
her, and staying healthy is important for her. But many
things slip in to sabotage a woman's good intentions:
childbirth, stress, a desk job, chocolate. And then one
day she looks in the mirror and says to herself, "This has
got to stop." She declares war on her fat, and suddenly
she's making salads and dreaming of brownies.

Losing weight is extremely hard because the dieter can't
simply give up food. For one thing, she needs it. For
another, it's everywhere. She has to shop for it, prepare it
for meals, and pack it in lunches. And if no one else in

the family is trying to lose weight, chances are she's packing temptation into a brown bag every day.

That's where you come in. You can help her by not bringing more temptation home. It's a lot easier on her diet if you take the kids out for ice cream than if you bring home a carton of the stuff. You can encourage her by praising her successes. She wants to look nice for you, so notice when she's lost weight and tell her how good she looks. Be her number one fan and root for her all the way to the diet finish line, and you'll both be happy with the results.

worth thinking about

▶ **Whenever possible** try to eat what she eats. Don't request she bake cookies or serve you fattening foods for dinner. Help her avoid diet disaster.

▶ **If you are** a snacker, keep your stash of treats at work and snack there so she doesn't have them close by in the cupboard to tempt her.

▶ **Exercise with her.** This can be anything from joining a co-ed sports team to an evening walk. The exercise and the time spent together will be beneficial to you both.

> *Whether you eat or drink or whatever you do, do it all for the glory of God.*
> 1 Corinthians 10:31, NIV

29

question
▼
How can you help your wife master her fears?

Some of your wife's fears are actually cute, and they make you smile. You're happy to kill spiders on her behalf or hold her tight during a thunderstorm. But the kind of fear that comes from self-doubt is another story. You want her to try, to accomplish things, and to feel good about herself. You want her to be successful and happy. How can a husband cut his wife free from the fears that hold her down and then help her soar?

answer
▼

The best way you can help your wife overcome her fears is by building up her confidence. When she's afraid to try something new, whether it's applying for a job, running a marathon, or simply getting out and meeting the neighbors, a woman's fears often stem from a lack of self-confidence. She may think, *I'm probably not good enough. What if I fail? What if I get rejected?*

Women are good talkers. They can easily build up someone else with words of encouragement, but they can as easily tear themselves down with all kinds of negative talk. Maybe your wife failed at something once and no one told her she could pick herself up and try again. Maybe she reached out to someone and was rejected. Maybe she doesn't see herself as deserving of good things. Whatever the root cause of her fear and doubt, you can find it and help her destroy it. You have the power to reset her thinking. When you, the most important person in her life, believe in her and encourage her to try, it sends the clear message that she is capable of more than she realizes. Knowing you're with her assures her that she's not alone. There's strength in numbers, and your support and encouragement will give her mental and emotional strength and will up her bravery quotient.

worth thinking about

▶ List her strengths. Deep down she suspects she's capable. Your verbalizing it will confirm her suspicions.

▶ Don't make light of her fears, even if they seem silly to you. They're very real to her.

▶ Remember those bicycle training wheels? Think of yourself as the human equivalent, and give her the support of your presence whenever possible. Attend intimidating events with her and applaud her success. Soon she'll have the confidence to race along on her own.

> *There is no fear in love, but perfect love casts out fear.*
> 1 John 4:18, NRSV

question

How does the gift of your time support your wife?

Your wife has your love and support. She knows that. But sometimes, when she wants your time, you can't help wondering why. Some of the things she wants you to do with her seem more female-friendly than guy-friendly. Surely she doesn't need you to accompany her on that one particular errand. And does she really want you to sit down and watch that chick flick with her? What is she really asking for when she asks for your time?

answer

She's asking for you, of course. She understands the value of time and the importance of investing it in things that really matter. And what matters most to her is your relationship. She needs to know you feel the same way.

When you give her the gift of your time, you are sending the message that she is the most important person in your life. You are giving her the most valuable thing you own, something that can't be renewed, something you will never get back or be able to make more of. There is no amount of gold, no stock, no diamond on earth that can compare to that. When you take time to do something thoughtful for her, you tell her she's worth the effort. When you do things with her, you make her feel good about herself. Your presence in her life makes her feel loved and secure. Your willingness to give up time for her that you would otherwise have spent on yourself shows her you value her and makes her feel loved.

Time spent together keeps you connected. It buys closeness and trust, and it gives her confidence in herself as a woman. Your gift of time reassures her that if she needs something she'll be able to count on you. After all, how can she not feel valued when you, her husband, lavish something so precious on her? If you want to make a wise investment, invest time in your wife.

worth thinking about

▶ **Whether it's a date** night or a home-repair afternoon, set aside some specific times where you make yourself available for whatever your wife needs.

▶ **It's easy** to get busy, but prioritize your schedule in a way that puts family first. Consult your wife before accepting invitations or making commitments, not because you need to ask permission, but because you want to work as a team and spend your time wisely.

▶ **When giving** your time, don't give grudgingly. God isn't the only one who loves a cheerful giver. Your wife appreciates one, too.

> *Being a husband is a whole-time job.*
> Arnold Bennett

31

question

What if your wife becomes more successful than you?

You want to see your wife succeed. Still, camped at the back of your mind is the concern that she may out-succeed you, and you're not sure how you'll feel about yourself as a man if that happens. These days a wife can have a better job than her husband and bring in a bigger salary. She may find creative success that puts her on the map and him in her shadow. How does a husband rejoice in his wife's success and still feel confident?

answer

The secret to enjoying your wife's success is to remember that you are not two people who are competing against each other. You are a team, and her success doesn't diminish yours. Her success *is* yours. When it comes to accomplishment, there is no his and hers. There is only ours. No person achieves in a vacuum. There is always a support team providing advice, physical help, and emotional support. You will never see an award show where the winner accepts her trophy and then quietly sits down. She always has a list of people to thank for putting her where she is.

You are an integral part of your wife's success picture. You help make it happen. When your wife does well, you both reap the benefits. She's happy, and that's good for your relationship. Perhaps her success brings monetary reward, and that gives you financial freedom. Benefits like these are great, but this issue goes far beyond benefits. Leaving behind your concern over who is more successful is the first step on a very high road.

Talent is a gift from God, and when you encourage your wife to use hers, you're assisting Him in helping her become the woman He meant her to be. As you concentrate on being a loving husband and the man God has called you to be, you won't have to worry about how to cope with your wife's success. You'll be too busy rejoicing with her.

worth thinking about

▶ Feel free to brag about your wife's accomplishments to others. This will keep you enthusiastic about her success.

▶ If tempted to feel jealous or insecure, remind yourself that you had the wisdom to pick her and that this amazing woman is yours.

▶ Make a habit of celebrating any time either of you accomplishes something. This will keep the good feelings going and will allow you both to celebrate no matter who is doing well.

> *Competition between God's servants is illogical for many reasons: We're all on the same team.*
> Rick Warren

question

How can you help her feel comfortable with your family?

You love your wife, you love your family, and you want them both to love each other. But you're not quite sure how to make that happen. What can you as a husband do to help your wife transition into your family? How can you make her feel at home with the people who are going to be such an important part of your life together? What can you do to help her feel like part of the family rather than an outsider?

answer

Fitting into a new family can feel overwhelming to a wife. Everyone but her, the newcomer, has a history together. Her only link to these people is you. With time she'll find common interests and start building shared memories, but while she and your family are moving into that more familiar territory, you can serve as her safe escort.

Support her with your presence. When you visit family members, don't wander off to work on your brother's car or duck into the den to check out the game and leave her alone to make conversation with your parents or other siblings—at least not until she feels comfortable with that. While she's still finding her feet, she needs you to translate remarks that may seem cryptic or help her understand your family's unique sense of humor. Having you at her side will do much to put her at ease. Help her build bridges by letting other family members know of interests or hobbies they might share.

This not only paves the way for your wife to establish friendships, but it also gives your relatives a tool with which to reach out to her. And always remember the importance of your touch. When you take her hand or put an arm around her shoulder, she'll be reminded that you're there with her and for her and will reassure her. Give her a secure launchpad, and before you know it, she'll be a beloved part of your family.

worth thinking about

▶ Try to attend important family functions so your wife can become a part of things and start forming bonds and building memories.

▶ If you have sisters, encourage them to invite your wife when they have female-friendly home parties. This can help her feel accepted and will build friend-ships.

▶ Since every woman is different, ask your wife what you can do to make her feel at home with your relatives. Then make sure you do what she asks.

> *Wherever you go, I will go; wherever you live,*
> *I will live. Your people will be my people.*
> Ruth 1:16, NLT

question

▼

What reassures your wife that she still has your heart?

You are your wife's knight in shining armor, her super-hero, the person she turns to first and always. You want her to feel safe and confident with you. But every woman has insecurities and times where she's unsure of herself. Even Lois Lane, who had Superman, had her off days. So your wife will probably have times when she needs reassurance. What can you say and do that will assure her that your love is steadfast and that your life together is secure?

answer

▼

The most reassuring thing for a married woman is proof that her husband still loves her, proof that she won't wake up one morning and find herself abandoned. Your faithfulness and steadfast presence reassure your wife that she doesn't have to worry she'll lose you. She needs to know that you love and accept her no matter what and that you'll always be there for her. She knows enough history, and she's seen enough movies and read enough books, to know that storybook weddings don't always evolve into happily-ever-after marriages. And in a culture where youth and beauty reign supreme, it is not hard to see how a wife can sometimes worry that she isn't enough. But when home is your favorite place to hang out, it reassures your woman that she is still number one in your life. When you walk through the door and greet her with a kiss, she knows she's loved.

She's not so naive as to think you won't look at other women, but it reassures her when you tell her she's the only one you need. Your dependable presence, your smile, your words of love will reassure her that although marriages around her may crumble, yours is solid. When you make your home and your life together a priority, your wife can rest confidently in your love.

worth thinking about

▶ If your wife has made a mistake, be sure to tell her you love her when you're making up. It will reassure her that you're there for her, even when she's not perfect.

▶ When you notice a nice-looking woman, don't comment on how attractive she is. It's never reassuring to a wife to hear her husband admire another woman.

▶ No matter how the day has gone, end every one with a good-night kiss and an "I love you."

> *Be happy with the wife you married when you were young.*
> Proverbs 5:18, CEV

34

question

▼

What is the most important way you protect your wife?

As a man, what you most want to do for your wife is to protect her. You're the one with the muscles and the strength, and you are more than happy to use them in her service, doing battle against all manner of bullies and villains. But one thing tops the list of areas where she needs protection. It's more vital than physical, financial, or emotional protection. What is the most important way you as a husband protect your wife?

answer

▼

The most important way you protect your wife is spiritually. She feels safest when she knows that she is in your hands and that you are in God's hands. Your wife can rest easy during any decision-making process when she knows that you'll consult God about that decision. She can feel confident in your leadership as a husband knowing that you are not leading in your own strength alone; rather, you are depending on a power greater than yourself.

Even with your mental and physical strength, there are some things you as a man simply can't do. You can't be with her every moment of the day. You can't protect her every second. But God can. When you pray for your wife, you protect her mentally, emotionally, and physically. By getting her to safe ground in the spiritual realm, you take better care of her than if you patrolled your house day and night.

When you set an example by taking your family to church, when you practice what you preach and live a life governed by God, you are giving your whole family a moral compass that can guide them through anything. By all means, offer your bravery and your strength to your wife. God made you big and strong for a reason. But don't forget that the most important battles you'll ever fight on her behalf will always be in the spiritual realm.

worth thinking about

▶ Set aside time each day to conference with God, telling Him your family needs and asking for wisdom as a husband.

▶ Pray with your wife when she's worried or anxious. Put your arm around her when you pray to reassure and comfort her.

▶ Find a church that both you and your wife can be excited about attending. Help her establish friendships. Make sure she feels connected before you commit to any involvements that will leave her sitting alone during church. If you can't both feel connected and happy, keep looking until you find a church where you can.

> *Our struggle is not against flesh and blood, but against the rulers, against the authorities, against the powers of this dark world and against the spiritual forces of evil in the heavenly realms.*
> Ephesians 6:12, NIV

35

question

How can you protect your wife emotionally?

Your wife has a tender heart, and emotion plays a large part in who she is and how she thinks. You love to see her happy, and when she's hurt or sad, you feel sad, too. You realize you can't protect her from ever feeling sad, but you'd like to spare her as much unhappiness as possible. How can you as a husband protect your wife in an area where she is particularly vulnerable, the area of emotions?

answer

Most women want to please and are not fond of confrontation. And because they want to please, criticism can be especially painful. One of the best ways you can protect your wife emotionally is by making a habit of being her protector when the two of you are out together. You've probably seen old movies where an irate husband let another man know, "You can't talk to my wife like that." This may seem cliché, but the principle behind it is still timely. A bully may have no problem intimidating a woman, but let a man step in front of her, and the bully often backs down.

You are your wife's wall of protection, and when other people see you watching out for her feelings, they'll be more careful how they treat her. If someone has said something hurtful or insulting to your wife, you as her husband have every right to suggest that person apologize. If a difficult person in your wife's life hurts her constantly, your wife may want you to be the buffer between them. The woman whose husband does nothing in the midst of confrontation feels abandoned, but the woman whose man will defend her can rest secure in the knowledge that she has an advocate. Your wife wants you to be her advocate. When you watch out for her feelings you're not only protecting her, but you're also deepening your relationship because she will appreciate you even more than she already does.

worth thinking about

▶ **If your wife** has a difficult family member to deal with, offer to be the go-between and relay messages or offer to be present with her when she's with this person so you can step in if she's attacked.

▶ **Encourage your wife** to have light contact with the people in her life who are hurtful.

▶ **Sometimes the worst** offender can be you. Make a habit of speaking to your wife in love. When you're angry, don't throw her flaws at her. Remember how important she is to you, and treat her accordingly.

> *When you invest in protecting your wife, you are making a statement about her value to you.*
> Dennis Rainey

question

In this modern age does your wife need your protection?

answer

I promise to love, guide, and protect you as Christ does His Church, and as long as we both are alive.

Christian Wedding Vow

question

How can you guard your relationship and keep it strong?

What you and your wife have is special. It is built on a unique combination of personalities, talents, and interests. Your marriage is a treasure of teamwork and support unlike any other relationship you'll ever have. Like all treasure, however, it needs guarding. How on earth, in a society that seems to be hard on marriages, does a man do that? How can you keep alive that special relationship you have with the woman you love?

answer

Think of your relationship as valuable art in a fine-art museum and of yourself as the head of security, assigned to keep it safe. As head of security, you are going to house that art behind a glass case where careless passersby can't break it and where intruders can't slip in and steal it. That locked case may seem unnecessary to the honest and responsible museum visitor, but you, as head of security, know it's necessary because not everyone who comes to the museum is honest or responsible. Neither is everyone who will pass through your lives as a couple, so your marriage needs a protective barrier. You build that by setting boundaries around yourselves. Those boundaries say: "No one is allowed to trample the intimate circle where my wife and I love and communicate. No one is allowed to enter and pull us apart. This is where it gets exclusive, where there is room for only two people: my wife and me."

By drawing lines that no one—not your boss, not your mother, not your best friend—can cross, you keep out people who might harm the relationship. You also protect yourself from stumbling off into the dangerous territory of temptation. Those borders honor the relationship by demanding exclusivity. They remind you that you chose the one you love and that now you must love the one you chose. By respecting the boundaries, you respect the relationship and keep it safe.

worth thinking about

▶ **Agree with your wife** on specific lines that neither of you will cross, starting with family. Don't allow either of your families unlimited access into your lives.

▶ **Friendship also needs** boundaries. Neither of you should cultivate close friendships with the opposite sex that can't be shared by both of you.

▶ **A job is good,** so is having a career. But you married neither. Put your marriage before both. Play is important, too, but always remember to play more together than apart.

> That's why a man leaves his father and mother and gets married. He becomes like one person with his wife. Then they are no longer two people, but one. And no one should separate a couple that God has joined together.
>
> Matthew 19:5–6, CEV

37

How does your wise money management protect your wife?

You understand the connection between money and success. You work hard to earn that paycheck, and you have big dreams for how to spend it. And you figure that as long as you're keeping up with paying the bills, you're doing all you need to do to take care of your wife. But are you? How does the way you manage your money actually protect your wife? Is there a philosophy you as a husband should embrace when it comes to managing money?

answer

The best philosophy to embrace is Benjamin Franklin's—a penny saved is a penny earned. Money is a powerful tool that can enable you to do all kinds of good things when you handle it carefully. As with any tool, however, if you get careless with it, someone can get hurt. Money mistakes can cost a good night's sleep, a good credit rating, and even your wife's trust. The decisions you as a husband make regarding spending money affect not only you, but also your wife. When you avoid the trap of credit card debt, you not only save your own skin, but you also save hers. You save her from the stress of dealing with creditors, and you save her from much worry also. As the keeper of the home, your wife sees where all those quickly vanishing dollars go: groceries, school clothes, football uniforms, yearbooks. When you slip up financially, she's often the one who has to juggle the dollars. But when you plan for the future by having money in savings for emergencies, when you refuse to risk family savings on get-rich-quick schemes, and when you're careful with how you spend your money, she can enjoy peace. Nothing terrifies a woman more than hearing the wolf howling at the door. When you resist the temptation to spend money you don't have, you're actually keeping the door to your financial house wolf-proof and allowing your wife to sleep at night, confident that she's safe.

worth thinking about

▶ **It's easy** to justify buying practically anything. When you consider purchasing a big-ticket item, before you tell yourself why you need it, ask yourself how the purchase will affect your family's budget and lifestyle.

▶ **Set financial goals** with your wife, and come up with a plan for how you can work together to meet those goals.

▶ **Financial expert** Dave Ramsey suggests keeping the equivalent of three to six months' paychecks in your savings account. This will not only help you in emergencies, but it will also give you and your wife peace of mind.

> *A big part of being strong financially is that you know where you are weak and take action to make sure you don't fall prey to the weakness.*
> Dave Ramsey

question

How can you watch out for your wife when you travel together?

Travel can be an adventure, whether you're seeing distant lands or simply going home for the holidays. While going places is fun, some kinds of travel may actually bring an element of physical risk while others may offer emotional stress. Going somewhere together can offer you myriad ways to protect your wife. Some you probably already do just because you're a good husband. Some you're probably aware of, but others may come as a surprise to you.

answer

You can do many things as a husband to protect your wife, simple things that will enable her to enjoy the adventure. One big thing you can do is save up enough vacation money to invest in lodging at nice motels in safe neighborhoods. Ending a day on the road or a long plane flight at a motel or hotel with good security will help her feel safe and help her to sleep well. And speaking of sleep, women like to stop for some. When a man gets in travel mode, he often wants to push on through to his destination. Women, on the other hand, like to stop for breaks, like to look at the scenery, like to rest. As a guy, you figure that you can rest when you get there. But your wife can be exhausted and sick by the time you reach your destination if you push too hard. When you allow rest time along the way, you'll protect both her health and yours. You also can protect your wife's sanity by avoiding exposing her to unnecessary risks, and generally listening when she has concerns or worries. No matter how well you plan, you can encounter problems, even dangers. That is why the most important way to protect your wife when traveling is to entrust yourselves to God's care every day. He alone can see what lies around the bend. By asking Him for wisdom and guidance, you can avoid trouble and gather great memories.

worth thinking about

▶ **Listen to your wife.** If she's feeling nervous staying in a certain neighborhood or at a particular campground, respect her fears and adjust your plans.

▶ **Drive carefully**—don't tailgate, don't speed. Nothing is more nerve-racking for the person in the passenger seat than having to endure riding with a driver who takes risks.

▶ **Don't forget** to pray together before you begin a trip. This will help you remember that God is with you in any situation and any location.

> *The world is a book, and those*
> *who do not travel read only a page.*
> Saint Augustine

39

question

What small things help make your wife feel safe?

Maybe it comes from having read Nancy Drew books as a girl, maybe she's easily influenced by what she sees in the movies, or maybe she's just seen enough in the news to make her wary. Whatever the source, your wife is very aware that it's a big, bad world out there. Where you love adventure, risk, and danger, she prefers fun, coziness, and safety. How can you as a husband give her that feeling of safety she needs?

answer

Well, Pilgrim, you don't have to be John Wayne to make your wife feel safe, and you don't need the fighting skills of a superspy. You simply have to care, be there, and be aware. Your presence may not seem like much to you, but it's hugely reassuring to her. She feels safe when she knows you're on guard duty. If she hears a noise in the night she can wake you up, and you'll investigate. She knows that with you around she doesn't make an easy target. Your safety precautions are also reassuring.

Your wife can rest easy when she sees you working to keep your home safe. When your house is in good repair and your doors have strong locks, she won't have to worry about burglars or rapists. Seeing you check every night to make sure the doors are locked has the same emotional effect on your wife as if she looked outside her window and saw a patrol car parked at the curb. That small action tells her that someone is watching over her. And not just anyone, but the man she loves. She reaps a double benefit. She's able to feel safe both physically and emotionally, secure in her home and secure in your love.

You don't have to slay dragons or fight off Viking hordes to be a good protector. Just show your concern for the big stuff in small preventive measures, and you'll make John Wayne proud.

worth thinking about

▶ **Take safety** preventive measures. Install dead-bolt locks, check your smoke alarms on a regular basis to make sure they're working, and get snow tires before the winter storms hit. These small things keep your family safe and reassure your wife.

▶ **Ask your wife** what you can do to help her feel safe. Then be open to doing what she needs.

▶ **Passing up** a candy bar or a second piece of pie may feel like a small thing, but doing it helps you stay fit and healthy, and increases the chances that you'll be around to protect your wife for a long time.

> *The husband is to regard the wife as the weaker vessel, and thus give her honor, support and protection.*
> Charles E. Orr

question

Whose side should you take when she's upset with someone?

As far as you're concerned your wife is close to perfect, but even women who are close to perfect can some-times handle situations imperfectly. Even the most agreeable of women can have a disagreement. And there are times when every woman, no matter how understanding she is, gets her feelings hurt. This can be especially hard for a husband if the person who did the hurting is a friend or relative. What do you do? Whose side do you take?

answer

The answer to this is not as difficult as it may seem: you take your wife's side. This can be hard if the person she's upset with is someone close, like your mother. You love your wife, you love your mom, and you would probably rather have your toenails pulled off than get in the middle of a problem between the two women you care most about in the world. But you and your wife are a separate unit, and as her husband you need to make sure that others respect her and treat her kindly. Your mom may think your wife is a terrible housekeeper, but it is not your mother's house. It's yours and your wife's. You may have a friend or relative who feels the need to put your wife in her place. Don't allow that. Let other people know that anyone who attacks your wife attacks you as well.

By taking her side, you show your wife that you are her advocate and protector and that you're there for her no matter what. There may be times when she gets offended unnecessarily, or when she is completely in the wrong. But no matter how wrong she is, you can still be on her side by protecting her from unkind words and awkward situations. Happy is the woman who knows that, no matter what, her husband will always be in her corner.

worth thinking about

▶ **Inform friends,** relatives, or coworkers who might be antagonistic that to attack your wife is to attack you. You don't need to be adversarial about it; simply give potential offenders a heads-up.

▶ **Escort your wife** from disagreements that are escalating into war, and don't subject her to situations where she won't be welcome.

▶ **When your wife** is in the wrong, remind her that she has your love and support, but help her come up with ways to fix the problem. You might even offer to undertake peace negotiations. Support doesn't always mean agreement, but it does mean you want her best.

The union of husband and wife merges two persons in such a way that little can affect one without affecting the other.
Commentary, *New Life Application Bible*

41

What can you do to help your wife stay healthy?

Your wife is the greatest thing in your life, and you want to keep her around as long as possible. And one of the surest ways to do that is to help her stay healthy. You know she'll not only live longer if she maintains a healthy body, but she'll also feel better and have a better quality of life. As her friend and lover, you want that for her. But how can you protect her health without being bossy or coming across as critical?

answer

Your wife needs to stay healthy, not only for you but for herself as well. But sometimes she can get so busy taking care of everyone else that she neglects her own health needs. Somewhere along the way she may have picked up habits that aren't good for her. Perhaps they are habits that you share, like smoking. In cases like that, the best way you can protect her is to change yourself and invite her to join you. When you lead the charge in the fight for a more healthful lifestyle, she will be inspired to join in.

It can be hard to make changes, and even harder to admit the need for those changes, so if you see a need, lovingly suggest healthy lifestyle alternatives, reminding your wife how much she means to you and how you want to grow old together. If you do so, she'll find it hard to get mad at you—or at least to stay mad at you. Encouraging her to get regular checkups will help her maintain good health. Being there for her emotionally when a checkup reveals something worrisome will do much for her mental state, and that will help her on the health home front as well. Your example and support mean more than you realize, and they can be key to protecting your wife's health.

worth thinking about

▶ Encourage your wife to stay fit by keeping your family's lifestyle active. Limit the couch-potato time. Make dates with your wife that involve doing something active that you enjoy together.

▶ Help your wife make a habit of taking vitamins. Women can often experience deficiencies in vitamins and minerals that affect both their health and their outlook on life.

▶ When your wife has to visit the doctor for test results that could be scary, go with her. Your support is always key to her health.

> *He who enjoys good health is rich,*
> *though he knows it not.*
> Italian Proverb

question

When does your wife *not* need your protection?

Have you ever rushed into a situation, ready to take the bullet for your wife, only to find she doesn't want you throwing yourself in front of her? Maybe you've stepped up to take on something or someone difficult and had your wife inform you, "I can do it myself." This can be a mystifying and frustrating experience. How is a husband to know when to back off and let his woman fight her own battles?

answer

This can be tricky, but here's a hint: when in doubt, stay out. Oh, you never have doubts? Well, then, here's another way to know when to leave your shining-knight shield behind. If your wife is dealing with nonthreatening situations and familiar problems or people, she probably can handle herself fine. Yes, she wants your emotional support. Always. But chances are, she wants to run her own game plan in sticky situations with her family or issues with her boss or coworkers. And unless she asks you to step in, she probably doesn't want you to protect her from herself in any financial matters. You may worry she's going to make a complete mess of the checkbook if you don't save the day. But if she's got it all under control, your stepping in will only step on her toes.

She loves knowing that you're there for her, her shield of protection against a hard world, but she is a person in her own right, with her own strengths and skills, and as your wife she wants to stand equal and pull her share of the load. She wants you to be there for her, but she's got more inner strength than you may realize, and sometimes she'd rather you just be there with her, applauding her strength and cheering her on.

worth thinking about

▶ **If you're not** sure what the boundaries are, ask your wife in what arenas she feels safe to fight her own battles.

▶ **Compliment her** when she insists on taking care of a difficult situation on her own and succeeds.

▶ **Don't feel** that you're not doing your part as a husband when you allow your wife to fight some of her own battles. She might outlive you, and being able to take care of herself will be a good skill to have.

> *Life affords no greater pleasure than that of surmounting difficulties.*
> Samuel Johnson

43 question

What makes you a hero in your wife's eyes?

The Medal of Valor, the Purple Heart, Most Valued Player, Olympic gold, the Heisman trophy, the Above and Beyond Citizen Honor—these all are the rewards of heroes, the stuff of dreams. What man doesn't want to be a hero, especially to his wife? No matter what praises you receive, what awards you win, you look first to your love and listen for her applause. You want to be her hero. What accomplishments and brave deeds will make her see you in that light?

answer

If you should happen to rescue a child from a burning building your wife would be proud, but you may be surprised to learn that you don't necessarily have to accomplish daring feats to be a hero in her eyes. When you show mercy to someone desperately in need of it, when you offer forgiveness and comfort rather than harshness and rejection to a child who has disappointed you, you become your wife's hero. When she sees you taking time to help people in need even though your own schedule is busy, she bursts with pride.

It is a thrill for your wife to see you reflecting the love of God to other people every day in everyday ways: helping someone move, stopping to change a tire for someone stuck by the side of the road, or letting her volunteer you as the neighborhood handyman. That kind of thing may sound mundane and not very brave or manly, but that is the kind of quiet strength a woman really admires. She wants you to achieve your goals and reach your highest dreams.

Bravery and self-sacrifice are the marks of a hero, but remember, your wife may have a different definition of bravery than you do. You may never face enemy fire or have an opportunity to rescue someone from physical danger, but when you have the courage to stand up for what's right, when you give of yourself, you will be her hero.

worth thinking about

▶ **When it comes** to opportunities to be a hero, think small. If you only look for big ways to live a noble life, you may miss a lot of opportunities to do something great.

▶ **Don't tell** your wife what you've done. Talking about good deeds takes away their shine. Let her see you in action or hear about it from someone else. There's no need to brag about yourself. Your deeds will say it all.

▶ **Be true** to your own convictions, and keep the man in the mirror happy. You'll be sure to win your wife's admiration as well.

> *God loves you and has chosen you as his own special people. So be gentle, kind, humble, meek, and patient.*
> Colossians 3:12, CEV

question

▼

What does your wife need to know to feel confident?

You believe in your wife's capabilities. Sometimes you believe in them more than she does. You want to see her try new things and tackle challenges with confidence, and when she's lacking in confidence you'd like to help her find more. You're not sure exactly how to do that, though. What makes a person confident? Where can a woman find this important attitude? Is there a way a husband can help his wife gain it?

answer

▼

Confidence is a learned attitude, which means it can be taught, and there are three important things your wife needs to know. First, she needs to realize that she doesn't have to depend on her strength alone, that God is always with her, ready and able to lead and guide her. When you help her keep sight of that fact, you're giving her a firm foundation on which to build her confidence. How can a woman be timid when she knows God is with her?

Second, she needs to know that she has your support, that you're behind her, rooting for her success. Think about the importance morale plays in keeping a soldier fighting or a team player working hard at his game. They understand people are behind them, rooting for them and counting on them, and that spurs them on to be and do more. You have that same ability to build your wife's morale and spur her to push on toward the goal.

The final thing she needs to know is that failing is not the end of the world, that you'll still be there for her, and that no one will think less of her for having tried. And when she succeeds, you both can rejoice in her accomplishment. And nothing builds confidence like success, so encourage your wife to try. With each success she'll gain more confidence, and soon she'll be off and running.

worth thinking about

▶ **Help your wife** build confidence by celebrating her successes. When you acknowledge her success, you remind her that she is a capable woman.

▶ **When your wife** has times of doubt, you can reassure her by reminding her of both God's faithful guidance and her successes in the past. There's nothing like past successes to inspire confidence for future endeavors.

▶ **Pray with your wife** when she's considering a new adventure and ask God to guide her. Spiritual assurance is the root of confidence.

> *I can do everything through Christ,*
> *who gives me strength.*
> Philippians 4:13, NLT

45

question

How can you prove she is your number one priority?

Your wife is the number one person in your life. You would move mountains for her, swim oceans, and even give up Sunday night football, although you hope it never comes to that. You want her not only to feel valued but also to realize that no other person or passion could ever take her number one spot in your heart. What can you do to prove to her how much you love and value her?

answer

The key word is *do*. Yes, a woman needs to hear how much her man loves her, so don't stop talking. Just add action to the mix. Your wife wants to see that she's important to you. Words of love with no behavior to back them up ring false, but when your behavior matches your declaration, you have irrefutable proof of how important she is to you. Women are very good observers. A wife hears a husband say she means the world to him, and then she watches as he makes selfish decisions or rushes to help other people while needs at home get ignored. She draws her own conclusions. When he backs out on yet another date night claiming he's just too tired, she sees that something is not adding up.

On the other hand, a wife sees her husband consider her feelings when making important decisions that will affect her, and she knows she matters. When he guards the time they spend together from the onslaught of a busy calendar, she sees clearly that she is the top priority in his life. Your wife understands that she can't be your whole life. She doesn't want you to give up your hobbies or your family and friends. She simply doesn't want to get put on a shelf and forgotten like some long-ago trophy you won. She wants to know that you value her as she values you. Love her like you mean it, and she'll never doubt you.

worth thinking about

▶ It is important to be a good neighbor and friend, but be a good husband first. Help your wife with projects around the house before volunteering somewhere else.

▶ Make a regular habit of spending time together, just the two of you. You show your wife that she's your top priority by not letting the demands of your career or other people squeeze her out.

▶ Respect her concerns. This is the number one way to show your wife how much you value her.

> *You don't want to wait until you are older to make your marriage a priority. Now is the time.*
> Jim Burns

question

What part do you play in building up your wife's self-esteem?

answer

He died for us so that, whether we are awake or asleep, we may live together with him. Therefore encourage one another and build each other up, just as in fact you are doing.

1 Thessalonians 5:10–11, NIV

question

How can you validate your wife's feelings?

Sometimes your wife's feelings are a mystery to you. You want to understand when she's upset or unhappy. You want to help her, to calm her fears, and to take away her worries. But there are times when your best efforts backfire. You say or do exactly what you think she needs, and then you get rewarded with a wifely accusation that you don't care about her feelings. This, of course, is untrue. You care. You just don't understand. You need to solve the mystery.

answer

The secret to validating your wife's feelings is to allow her to have them. Because you love her, your first instinct is to rush in and fix the problem, which means getting rid of those pesky unwanted feelings. This is especially true if they make no sense to you or make you uncomfortable. And tears? Oh, please, not tears. You're completely at a loss when she cries. But tears and feelings are a big part of being female, and your wife wants you to allow her to be who she is and feel as she does. No strings attached. She doesn't want you to dismiss her feelings as unimportant, which is what she thinks you're doing when you try to pull her into a more happy state with remarks like "It's not that big a deal, hon," or "I think you're obsessing about this way too much." It may not be a big deal and maybe she is obsessing, but she still needs to cope with her feelings. And she needs you to understand that.

When you listen without criticism or advice, you offer her a safe haven in which she can be herself. When you resist the temptation to help her see the bigger picture by dismissing her feelings, you reassure her that you do care how she feels. And showing you care is the one true way to validate her feelings.

worth thinking about

▶ **When your wife** is talking about something she feels strongly about, ask concerned questions to show that you're not only listening but that you truly care.

▶ **Even if you** don't understand her point of view, be a good listener and be sympathetic.

▶ **Try not to** get frustrated when the way she feels makes no sense to you. Keep negative thoughts to yourself. If you have trouble doing this, remember that you'd want her to listen to you even if she didn't understand what was bugging you.

> *When people feel understood emotionally they feel cared for.*
> Gary Smalley

47

question

▼

How can you get your wife to appreciate her uniqueness?

You chose your wife because, of all the women you ever dated, you found her to be the most interesting and appealing. She's the one you just had to have. You love the way she's put together and the way she smiles. You appreciate her outlook on life and her sense of humor. In short, you think she's great. She doesn't always share your viewpoint. In fact, sometimes she can be unnecessarily critical of herself. How can you help her appreciate herself just the way she is?

answer

▼

Today's woman has trouble seeing. Magazines, movies, and TV can negatively affect her eyesight, blinding her with airbrushed images of "perfect" women and Barbie dolls racing across the big screen performing superhero feats. She then takes a peek in her mirror and, still blinded, thinks, *Yuck*. Maybe it's her nose. Too big. Maybe it's her hips. Too fat. Maybe it's her talent. Too small. She hates her straight hair. She wishes she had straight hair. If only, if only. And on and on it can go.

But you can help her adjust her eyesight to see all the good things about herself. Your admiration and assurances that she's just right can help her worry less about that extra pound she's imagining. She may have some days when her hormones are swinging downward, when it's hard to see anything good about herself. Those are the days when you can give her an emotional lift by reminding her of all the ways in which she's special. Women tend to pick themselves apart feature by feature and bit by bit. You can pull her back from that obsessive inspection and help her see the whole picture, the woman you fell in love with. By giving her your reassurance, your admiration, and your positive input, you will give her the aid she needs to see and appreciate her own uniqueness.

The best way you can help your wife is by improving her eyesight.

worth thinking about

▶ Pay for a professional photographer to take her picture (perhaps one who specializes in glamour shots). Then pick your favorite picture, get it framed, and put it on your desk at work or on your nightstand at home.

▶ When she bemoans her faults, don't dismiss her. Reassure her that you love her just the way she is.

▶ Take time to reminisce about what attracted you to her in the first place and why you think she's so special. This is one of the best things you can do to help her see herself in a positive light.

> *Thank you for making me so wonderfully complex! Your workmanship is marvelous— how well I know it.*
> Psalm 139:14, NLT

question

How can you help your wife grow as a person?

You don't want to ever grow stagnant. You want to always be moving forward. And you want your wife to grow right alongside you. Your hope for her is that she will continue to be both interesting and interested. You want to see her learn more about God and explore new ways of looking at the world. How can a man inspire his wife to keep reaching for new heights? How can he help her to blossom and grow?

answer

In order to grow, a wife needs both her husband's permission and his presence. For her to truly enjoy trying and doing new things, your wife must be able to rest in the knowledge that she has your blessing. This frees her to take time from her duties to enjoy developing as a person. It frees her to happily share what she's learned and accomplished. It gives her the security she needs to strike out.

Your presence during her growth period is equally necessary. No one likes to experience things in a vacuum. Your wife wants to know that she's not alone, that you are with her and interested in what she's learning and becoming. If you take an interest and ask questions, you'll encourage her all the more and help her maintain an excitement level about her life and activities. If you find things you can experience as a couple, you can both grow together. Discussing each other's thoughts and reactions to shared experiences gives you each a chance to learn and become someone new. Your encouragement as she explores her world, your support on the home front to enable her to learn, and your interest in what she discovers will all help your wife continue to grow as a person and will allow you to both enjoy the person she is becoming.

worth thinking about

▶ **If your wife** is timid in new situations, give her plenty of moral support. Help her meet and connect with new people so that she can establish rapport and maintain a foundation for building relationships.

▶ **Encourage your wife** to go back to school or to take continuing-education classes through her local parks department or nearby college campus. Offer to watch the kids so she can relax and enjoy her classes.

▶ **Water her talents** by budgeting money for her to attend seminars that will help her learn, grow, and pursue her dreams.

> *A good marriage is one which allows for change and growth in the individuals and in the way they express their love.*
> Pearl S. Buck

question

How does expressing your opinions tear down or build up your wife?

Your relationship with your wife is built on trust. She's the one person in the world you feel the safest with, the one person you can really be yourself around. It stands to reason that because you're so close, you should be free to say whatever you think. But there are ways and then there are ways for a husband to offer his opinion. How can you make sure that when you offer yours you'll be building up rather than tearing down?

answer

An opinion should be just that, simply another viewpoint to consider, but opinions take on more weight when delivered by someone a woman cares about. When they come from her husband, the man she trusts with her body, heart, and soul, opinions double in weight and can pack enough power to either pin her down or raise her up. She values your opinion, and she has the same desire to look good in your eyes that you have to look good in hers. If you frame your opinion in harsh words, you can cut her to the quick. If you share your thoughts honestly but kindly, you can be both truthful and helpful.

Yes, when she asks that common leading question about a certain pair of pants making her look fat she does want an answer, but she wants it carefully delivered. She doesn't need graphic comparisons to the Goodyear blimp. She simply needs to hear that she should probably try a different outfit. She wants to know that even when you tell her something unpleasant, you'll tell her as gently as possible to avoid bruising tender feelings. Hearing the truth is important, but hearing it said in love is vital. When you make a habit of doing that, she can rest secure in the knowledge that even though others may relish beating her over the head with bluntness, you will always take care to be kind.

worth thinking about

▶ **Before you verbalize** your opinion, give your delivery a quick mental check to make sure you're going to offer your input in a helpful and not hurtful manner.

▶ **Don't take** it personally when your wife listens to someone else's advice over yours. It doesn't mean she doesn't value your input. It simply means that, after sifting through her options, she picked a different one.

▶ **Sometimes it's wisest** to keep your opinion to yourself, especially in matters where it's based simply on taste or preference.

> *Kind words can be short and easy to speak,*
> *but their echoes are endless.*
> Mother Teresa

50

question
▼
How can you help her grow old gracefully?

Your wife seems to notice those little lines and wrinkles much more than you do. You look at her and see the woman you love. You think she still looks great. A little older maybe, but so what? So are you. Aging is part of life, but it doesn't appear to be a part she's fond of. How can you help her ignore the jabs of Father Time, enjoy your life together, and grow old gracefully?

answer
▼

Your encouragement and admiration can't stop the aging process, but they will help her cope with the frustrations of getting older. She'll never be fond of those wrinkles and gray hairs, and she'll probably fight every new one that shows up. Knowing that you still find her attractive in spite of them will go a long way toward helping her accept that ever-changing face in the mirror. She may find herself frustrated that her body isn't as supple or flexible as it once was, but knowing you still appreciate every curve will be a comfort.

As you and your wife walk through the years, you can do it holding her hand and giving her comfort and assurance. Help your wife see the benefits of aging. There are so many things she can look forward to: chances to grow and to find new friends and hobbies, and opportunities to learn new things and help other people.

If you remind your wife that her true beauty is from within and that with each new year of experiences and opportunities she blossoms into a more fascinating woman, you'll help her realize that age is just a state of mind. Deal with the challenges of aging, of course, but concentrate on what is good, and turn your wife's focus that direction as well. You'll both benefit.

worth thinking about

▶ **Remind her** that wisdom comes with age. Tell her you appreciate her insights.

▶ **When she wants** to try new things, never throw cold water on her plans by suggesting she may be too old, even if you're worried she may get hurt. You'll hurt her more by discouraging her.

▶ **Make a habit** of always planning a new adventure, whether it's taking a trip, building a house, or sponsoring an orphan. Life gets better with each year when you keep it interesting.

> *We never give up. Our bodies are gradually dying, but we ourselves are being made stronger each day.*
> 2 Corinthians 4:16, CEV

51 question

▼

How does your spiritual maturity affect your wife's self-esteem?

You know it is important to grow spiritually. You see how growing close to God and learning to live by His principles raises your level of spiritual maturity and makes you a better man. You even see how that spiritual growth touches your relationship with your wife and makes you a better husband. But can your spiritual growth actually affect her self-image? And if that's the case, what can you as a husband do to affect it positively?

answer

▼

Your spiritual maturity touches everything you think, say, and do, which is exciting because that means you can look forward to becoming all that God intended you to be. It also means that you have the capability to help your wife also become everything God wants her to be as well. When you treat her as your helpmate, stamped with the image of God just like you, you demonstrate to her how valuable she is, not only in your eyes but in God's eyes, too. When you respect her talents as God-given and encourage her to use them, you allow her to see herself as a valuable human being and you build her confidence, enabling her to use those gifts.

An insecure husband might use his position of leadership as an excuse to become a dictator in his home. An immature husband might figure that Adam, as the first model of humanity, proved man was superior to everyone.

Your challenge as a mature husband is to realize that it isn't good for man to be alone, and that just as Eve was a gift to Adam, your wife is a gift to you. When you look at yourself as your wife's protector, you will gain her loyalty. When you see her through God's eyes and treat her accordingly, you will help her see herself correctly, and she'll appreciate what she sees.

worth thinking about

▶ **God gave Eve** to Adam to help him serve God working in the garden, not to be his personal servant. Likewise, He gave you your wife to help you do what you have been put here to do. Treat her as your trusted coworker.

▶ **Lead by example** and request rather than by demand and command.

▶ **Never use** biblical terms or principles as a prod to get cooperation. That isn't use; it's misuse. Kindness and consideration are still the best motivators in the world for a loving wife.

> *Eve was not taken out of Adam's head to top him, neither out of his feet to be trampled on by him; but out of his side, to be equal to him, under his arm to be protected by him, and near his heart to be loved.*
>
> Matthew Henry

52 — question

What can you do when
she puts herself down?

You think your wife is wonderful. But she doesn't always
agree. In fact, sometimes you are surprised at how
swiftly and brutally she can put herself down. It is easier for you to please her than it is for her to please herself. It seems there is always something she's unhappy
about. You hate to see her being unappreciative of how
God made her. Why does she put herself down, and
what should you, as a husband, do when she does?

answer

Men look in a mirror and say, "Hey, not bad," or "You've
still got it." Women look in a mirror and say, "Oh, no,
a zit!" or "I hate my hair." While you have probably
learned to cut yourself some slack, your wife may have
lost her scissors somewhere along the way. Her put-
downs spring from feeling frustrated because she isn't as
perfect as she would like to be. Who told her she had to
be perfect? Who knows? Maybe her mother. Maybe her
girlfriends. Maybe some marketer. Any of the above. All
of the above. But those put-downs are more than a ven-
tilation system for her insecurity or frustration over her
imperfections. They are also bait, designed to lure you
into rising to the challenge and assuring her that she's

just fine. She may say, "I hate my hair," but she is really asking, "You think it's nice, though, right?" She may moan, "How could I be so stupid?" but she is really asking, "I'm not stupid, am I?" She wants to be someone special. So remind her often that she is. Don't wait for her to put herself down. Head her off at the pass as often as possible. Shift her focus from what is negative, and encourage her to see and be thankful for what is positive. Help her to see everything that she is, and with time she will feel less frustrated and come to appreciate the good things about herself and worry less about the bad.

worth thinking about

▶ **Help pull her** away from the put-down pattern by encouraging her to play to her strengths and to quit fretting over what she can't change.

▶ **What you say** has power. Suggest she go a week without lamenting her faults. And, if you have been in the habit of pointing them out to her, pledge to put away your pointing stick.

▶ **If she is putting** herself down out of frustration or insecurity, help her come up with a plan to change the shortcomings that are bugging her. Feelings of incompetence can be cured by such positive life changes as taking continuing-education classes.

> *How shall we expect charity towards others,*
> *when we are uncharitable to ourselves?*
> Thomas Browne

question

▼

What attitudes and behavior build a foundation for physical intimacy?

Your wife is beautiful, and she's yours. You love her like crazy and can hardly keep your hands off her. And you don't want to. You want to enjoy years of intimacy with her. What, as a husband, can you do to ensure that happens? How can you maintain and increase the closeness you already have? What kind of attitude and behavior builds a solid foundation for lasting love and a great sex life?

answer

▼

Great sex grows out of a great relationship. And the best way to have a great relationship is to be a great guy. Your wife walked down the aisle carrying her heart to you. Of course you want to keep it healthy and happy because you love her, too. And as you make an effort to do that, you will reap an important side benefit: you will lay a solid foundation for intimacy.

When you speak to her with respect, when you avoid falling into the trap of taking her for granted—in short, when you treat her like a lover, a lover is what you will get in return. Do you compliment her on a great meal or thank her for making you a sandwich? Or do you say things like "Where's the mayo?" Lovers aren't critical.

They are too busy being besotted. Lovers praise and compliment. Lovers appreciate and desire the beloved. If you make a habit of appreciating your wife and desiring her smile, her laughter, and her company, you are going to have a willing partner when you desire her body.

When you pay attention to her during the day, she will be much more responsive when you go to her at night. Remember that women don't compartmentalize. Your wife won't shelve that unlovable behavior you exhibited earlier and come joyfully into your arms later when you are feeling amorous. But treat her like your beloved throughout the day every day, and she will be your beloved when you want to become physically intimate.

worth thinking about

▶ **Maintain an atmosphere** of love and acceptance in your home. When your wife feels loved she can freely give love.

▶ **Think back** to the things you did when you were dating, and make sure you continue to incorporate those things into your life as a married couple. It is easy to let the busyness of everyday life rob you of intimacy. Keep intimacy high on your priority list.

▶ **Keep learning.** Make sure you read a new how-to book on maintaining healthy relationships once a year. It will keep you on your game.

> *Men are stimulated by sight, while women are stimulated by attitudes and actions.*
> Jill Savage

question

▼

How can you make good use of a couch?

There it is, the best place in the house from which to watch the game, the perfect pod for an afternoon nap, a nice comfortable spot where you can kick off your shoes and morph into the proverbial potato. But it is so much more. Maybe you have seen that couch so much that you've forgotten another fun use for it. Perhaps it's time to take another look at that couch and think how you can use it to benefit your marriage.

answer

▼

It is easy to fall into routines, to get in the habit of walking into your house and seeing the furniture and trappings in the same old way. The fridge is where you go when you're looking for . . . something. The TV is what you park your tired self in front of after a long day at work. The couch is your favorite parking place. Or maybe the couch is the place you park your company. But what was it before you relegated it to such mundane duty? Think back to your courtship days. Ever spend some time on the couch, cuddling and watching a movie, kissing and sharing secrets? A couch is a great setting for a man wanting to create some sparks with his wife. It is an easy stage to set for romance. Lots of pillows, some fun goodies to eat on the coffee table nearby, romantic music on the stereo, and you're ready. Because it's soft, comfortable, and familiar, a couch is the perfect place to snuggle, the perfect place to relax, and even a great place to have a heart-to-heart talk or to make up after a fight. If you have a fireplace or woodstove nearby, so much the better. So take another look at that familiar piece of furniture, and instead of associating it with passive behavior, look at it as something you can use to be proactive in your marriage, as a great aid for romance and closeness.

worth thinking about

▶ Use the couch to give your wife a foot rub while you both share how your days went.

▶ Try putting the kids to bed early and enjoy a Friday night couch campout with popcorn and root beer, your favorite books, or a great DVD you can watch cuddled up together. Make sure you have lots of pillows and blankets.

▶ Spend an evening on the couch, just the two of you with no TV, and seduce your wife with love poems, kisses, and back rubs.

> *Every marriage needs a healthy dose of ongoing romance to add spice, delight, and fun to the relationship. It's not enough to just start out with a sizzling romance. You have to find a way to keep the romance alive as the months and years accumulate.*
>
> Nancy Wasson

question

What are the many things you say through touch?

Touch is a vital human need, and it has a language all its own. A man can say a lot to his wife using this non-verbal communication. Sometimes he doesn't even realize he is talking. Your wife knows exactly how you feel by the way you do or don't touch her. What are some of the things you say to her when you use this unspoken communication? How can you increase your touch vocabulary?

answer

Every touch you give your wife has its own special message. When you run a hand up her leg or place a kiss on her shoulder, you both know what you are asking. When you give her a quick peck on the cheek as you go out the door, she hears that you care, but, gotta go! Those are the obvious messages, and most men manage them just fine. Still, you can say much more.

Touch really is the language of love. It is romantic and exciting for women, and it keeps the fire burning inside them. Even if you are a man of few words, you can learn to say a lot with your hands. A grin and a tap on the tip of her nose when she says or does something amusing can tell her that you find her cute. Taking her hand when you're out to dinner assures her that you want to keep the romance alive. And when was the last time you raised her hand to your lips and kissed it? Yes, it's an old-fashioned gesture, but as far as most women are concerned, it never went out of style. A pat on the bottom when she says something saucy keeps you playful. A hand to the cheek before you kiss her good night or good morning tells her how much you treasure her. Touching your wife in new ways physically will open doors to new communication on other levels, too.

worth thinking about

- ▶ **If you are not** a touchy-feely kind of guy, start slowly. Try giving your wife an unexpected hug before dinner, and ask if you can help with anything.

- ▶ **Put your arm** around her at movies or concerts. You don't have to keep it there until it goes numb, but when you do pull it away, give her a kiss.

- ▶ **Touch her** often with no thought of its leading to physical intimacy. A wife appreciates it when her husband's language of touch doesn't always say "sex."

> *Loving touch makes the difference.*
> Everett Tetley

▼

How important is a good sexual relationship?

▼

Such is the ironical power of sex:
It lures us into a relationship that
offers to teach us what we need
far more—sacrificial love.

Philip Yancey

56

When is your wife most open to lovemaking?

Before you married her, your wife was a fascinating mystery girl. She still is, especially in matters pertaining to the bedroom. Her sexuality is far from straightforward. Instead, it runs much like a river, full of changing currents and unexpected turns. Just when you think you have it all figured out, you discover that you don't. Is there a formula that explains when a wife will welcome her husband's lovemaking? What puts her in the mood?

answer

If sexual drive could be graphed like a giant thermometer, your drive and your wife's drive would look distinctly different. Simply by anticipating sexual intimacy, the mercury in yours would shoot up, but the mercury in hers would rise much more slowly. That is because many elements combine to stoke the fire of her desire. That is because physical love for her is only part of the package. Her true treasure is emotional love. In the act of lovemaking, you delight in physical release while she delights in the emotional high. Yes, she enjoys physical release, but if she is not satisfied emotionally, she'll never find it.

If you want to drive her wild, turn the ignition long before you hit the bedroom. The best romancing you can do is to help her with her chores when she is overloaded rather than waiting until she's done with her work so that you can make your move. A generous man is a turn-on. She doesn't expect you to bring her flowers or to give her jewelry every time you want to make love, but she does want you to be generous with your time and your compliments. She wants to be wooed. After some kind words, some sweet gestures, and some soft lights following on the heels of some sacrifice—that is when your wife is most open to lovemaking because that is when she feels truly loved. She knows you don't want her for something. You want her. Period.

worth thinking about

▶ **It is hard** for your wife to get excited about lovemaking when she is tired. Don't wait until eleven o'clock at night when she has been up since five to take her in your arms.

▶ **Hormones can play** a big role in receptivity. Know your wife's hormonal cycle, and learn to read the signals.

▶ **Privacy is important** to women. Make sure when you pick a lovemaking spot that it is secluded so she can feel free to let herself go.

> *I slept, but my heart was awake, when I heard my lover knocking and calling: "Open to me, my treasure, my darling, my dove, my perfect one."*
> Song of Songs 5:2, NLT

57

question

▼

How can you get intimacy higher up on her priority list?

Intimacy with your wife is number one on your priority list. If you had to choose between skydiving and an afternoon of wild love with your wife, you would rather free-fall with her. If you had to choose between mountain climbing and loving your wife, you'd let the mountain wait. But even as much as she loves you, you are not sure that sexual intimacy ranks as high on her priority list. How can you move it up a notch or two?

answer

▼

It has been said that as humans we all run toward pleasure, so if you want your wife to be running toward your open arms, you will want to make sure that when she's there the experience is as wonderful for her as it is for you. Pleasure can be addicting. The more she enjoys your times of physical closeness, the more eager she will be to come back for more. If the experience is a hurried rush that barely raises her temperature, she won't be all that excited to repeat the experience on a regular basis. So think of this as a fun challenge, and work on raising her temperature.

A woman comes to lovemaking with high expectations, but those expectations aren't as hard to meet as a man may imagine. What your wife really wants is to see that you care about her enjoyment as much as you care about your own and that you're willing to take the time to give it to her. Making love with your wife is much like traveling with your wife. While you want to reach the destination, she wants to enjoy the trip. So don't rush her. When you take time for tenderness, and when you ask her what feels good and then make an effort to give it to her, she can enjoy the experience as much as you do.

worth thinking about

▶ **When you are** together, don't be too proud to ask for direction. Find out what is working for her and what isn't.

▶ **Don't insist** on her doing things that make her uncomfortable. You want her to be turned on being with you, not turned off.

▶ **Invest some money** in your physical relationship. Take her away once in a while for a night at a nice hotel, or give her a gift card to spend at her favorite lingerie store. Remember, you want intimacy to be pleasurable. Clothes and pretty trappings spell pleasure to most wives.

> *Let him kiss me with the kisses of his mouth—*
> *for your love is more delightful than wine.*
> Song of Songs 1:2, NIV

58

question

How can you sweep your wife off her feet?

You want to be your wife's romantic fantasy, the man of her dreams. You don't want lovemaking to be something she does because she has to or even because she wants to please you. You want her to crave you the way she craves chocolate. You want to be her leading man, her romance-novel hero, her favorite thrill. What can you do to sweep her off her feet?

answer

Your wife loves romance. And what better man to give it to her than you? Here is your opportunity to act like a movie star. This can be fun. Okay, you don't get to blow things up, but you do get the girl. Think about those swashbuckling heroes that women swoon over: bandits, pirates, and sheiks. What do they have in common? Their masculinity. A pirate has no problem kidnapping a beautiful woman and sailing off with her on his ship. A bandit is a bad boy who delights in stealing a kiss whenever he can. And a sheik? He's happy to pick up a woman, take her into his tent, and cover her with kisses.

This excessive masculinity is a tough job, but somebody's got to do it, and in your house that somebody is you. Sweep your wife off her feet with sensory overload. Have you ever noticed how, when she is setting the scene for romance, she pays attention to details? She lights a candle, puts on her prettiest nightgown, and dabs on perfume. You really only care about what is at the center of the scene: her. But she is into details, so as her own personal ravisher, become a detail man. Give her treats for all her senses. Whisper sweetly seductive promises in her ear, run your hands through her hair. Don't be afraid to be manly, and don't be afraid to do a little role-playing. She is more ready to play than you realize.

worth thinking about

▶ Pay attention to what raises your wife's temperature. Read some of the books she reads. Watch to see what romantic movie scenes or song lyrics make her sigh.

▶ Serenade her. There is something about her man pouring out his heart in song that turns a woman's heart to putty.

▶ Try some movie-hero moves like running your finger along her lips before kissing her or raising a glass to her and toasting your love. Romantic gestures are a woman's favorite adventure.

> *If I had the power to communicate only one message to every family in America, I would specify the importance of romantic love to every aspect of feminine existence.*
> James Dobson

question

What can a hug accomplish?

Remember how much hugging you did when you were dating? You loved wrapping your arms around that woman and pulling her close to you. It gave you a charge on many levels. Touching her was a thrill, and holding her was emotionally satisfying and reassuring. Yep, that babe was yours. But now that you're married you have moved on. A hug is what you give your mother or old friends who come to visit. What purpose does it serve with your wife?

answer

A hug can accomplish a lot, for both your wife and you. Hugging is good for your emotional health. God designed humans for closeness, and hugs are physical evidence of that closeness. Researchers suggest that human beings need four hugs a day for survival, eight hugs a day for maintenance, and twelve a day for growth. They remind you and your wife that when you married you came together as one, that you are now and for a lifetime connected—a duo, a team, a pair. A hug can reassure her that she is still your baby. It can remind her how safe she feels in your arms. Receiving hugs is not only good for your wife emotionally, but it is also good for her health. More frequent hugs have actually been linked to lower blood pressure in some women.

It's good for your health, too. Life can be stressful. Hugging is a good way to combat that stress. A simple hug keeps you connected. When you hug your wife, you receive a tangible reminder that you have someone in your life who cares for you and who is important to you. That hug sends you out in the world knowing that you are valuable to another person. It sends you out with the awareness that someone loves and is depending on you. Hugs reassure, recommit, and reconnect. Hugs keep you emotionally healthy, make your wife happy, and help you keep the connection between the two of you strong.

worth thinking about

▶ Think of a hug as an emotional vitamin, and make sure you and your wife get the recommended daily amount.

▶ Pick at least one time of the day, like in the morning before you leave for work, and designate it as hugging time.

▶ Always hug your wife when you're making up after a fight. This serves two purposes. It reassures her that you still love her, and it reminds you that you two are a lifetime team.

> *A hug is like a boomerang—*
> *you get it back right away.*
> Bil Keane

question

How can
you make
love fun?

It is easy to fall into habits and slip into ho-hum mode, but you do not want that for your marriage. You want the love relationship between you and your wife to be fun. You not only want to keep her, but you also want to keep her excited, about you. When it comes to love and love-making, what spells fun to a wife? How can you make love the exciting adventure for her that it is for you?

answer

Fun and play go hand in hand. If you make your wife your playmate, you can bring a whole new dimension to your relationship, both in and out of the bedroom. In fact, you can show physical love in places other than the bedroom. The proverbial bear rug or a blanket in front of the fireplace or in the kitchen, handy to the strawberries and whipped cream, can make a nice change. Fun for your wife is getting courted, so take her out and court her. Going to an amusement park and winning her a stuffed toy (or trying to win a stuffed toy) can make you both feel carefree and young again. It is not so much what you do but the fact that you try that wins you points as a husband.

Does she like to hike? Try a romantic rendezvous in the woods. Does she like to dance? Try a whirly waltz around the patio. Does she like to bicycle? Try a picnic basket and a bicycle built for two.

When you take time to think of little surprises, when you bring a sense of play into a busy, stressful life, you are saying that you care. You tell your wife, "There is no one I enjoy life with more than you." And when you inject a little fun into your relationship, it inspires her to do the same. Think about things your wife enjoys doing, and then try incorporating some aspect of them into your daily lives or your lovemaking, and you will boost the fun factor for both her and you.

worth thinking about

▶ **Catch your wife** by the hand as she walks by and pull her onto your lap. Whisper that you'd love to drizzle chocolate down her neck and lick it off. Or better yet, have an intimate chocolate fondue party and do exactly that.

▶ **Have a picnic** for two in bed once in a while with both your favorite treats.

▶ **Try organizing** a treasure hunt where she has to search for a love note and some small token of your affection. This can be enjoyable for her and fun for you to organize.

> *You cannot work at creating better lovemaking—*
> *you and your mate have to play at it.*
> Douglas E. Rosenau

question

What should you do when she's not in the mood?

Sexual intimacy is your favorite way to express your love, and if it were up to you, you and your wife would make love every day. But you are not always equally balanced when it comes to physical desire, and sometimes she isn't receptive when you try to initiate lovemaking. For you this can be confusing, frustrating, and even hurtful. What can you, as a loving husband, do when you want to be intimate and your wife simply isn't in the mood?

answer

The top thing you as a husband can learn to do when your wife says, "Not tonight," is to allow her the freedom to refuse. So many things can affect a woman's libido: hormones, physical exhaustion, or emotional hurt. If you have done something to offend her, you will have to backtrack, make it right, and restore her heart to its happy and receptive state. But if she is tired or her hormones are on a downward swing, she may simply need a chance to recharge her batteries. When your wife is not in the mood for physical love, sometimes what she needs most is a good dose of consideration. Maybe she needs help with her workload.

A woman can become emotionally drained taking care of her family, and as much as she loves to be with you, if she is drained emotionally, making love can feel like one more need she has to find the energy to meet. When that happens, the best thing you can do for her is to put her to bed early and tuck her in. Maybe she simply wants you to hold her and let her tell you her troubles.

When she is not in the mood, don't try to persuade her that she really is. She knows what she wants. Instead, give her an opportunity to tell you why she's not receptive. And give her the freedom to choose. By doing that, you will earn her gratitude and respect.

worth thinking about

▶ **When your wife** is not in the mood for love, don't pout. Instead, be gracious, give her a kiss, and tell her you love her.

▶ **Don't make sex** with your wife your only form of physical release. Get physical exercise and direct some of that sexual energy into worthwhile projects.

▶ **If you think** your wife is pulling away from you, ask her what's wrong. Resentment will dry up the well of physical love. Don't let it get a foothold in your relationship.

> *Love cares more for others than for self.*
> 1 Corinthians 13:4, THE MESSAGE

question

Where does your wife's family fit into the picture?

When you fell in love, you fell in love with just your wife. Then you married and realized you got a package deal: the woman you love came with a family. Now you have other people to consider when planning for holidays and birthdays. Sometimes you even have other people offering you unrequested advice. What happened to leaving mothers and fathers and cleaving to each other? Where do your in-laws fit into the family portrait that is you and your wife?

answer

Family is important, both the new one you are building and the extended ones that surround and support you as a couple. That is why it is important to establish boundaries, but it is equally important not to erect walls. Even though you and your wife are a separate unit, she still has strong ties to the people who cared about her long before you came on the scene. Her family helped shape her into the woman she is today, the woman you love.

While you two will make your own decisions and establish your own home, you'll also be enjoying the support of those people who care for your wife and who now care for you as well. You and your wife are at the center of your family picture, but the frame around you is made up of people who care about you. So as you look out at that family she wants to spend time with, don't see them as a nuisance or a threat to your marriage. See them instead as part of your network; see them as people interested in and working to help the two of you make a home together. Yes, you will be spending time with these people, maybe more than you originally anticipated, but you will also be building relationships that will benefit both you and your wife. Her family is her history, part of her identity, and even an integral part of her emotional support system. And as years go by, they will become yours, too.

worth thinking about

▶ **Establish times** for your immediate family to be together as well as times to include extended family. If you want to spend a particular holiday with only your wife, plan to gather with extended family prior to the big day.

▶ **Accept the fact** that your mother-in-law is your wife's number one adviser and that if you mess up as a husband, Mom will probably learn about it.

▶ **Remember birthdays**, and do things to get involved with your in-laws. This will help you establish your own relationship with them and make you feel like part of the gang.

> *The family was ordained by God before he established any other institution, even before he established the church.*
> Billy Graham

63

question

▼

Why does she spend so much time with her girlfriends?

It seems like she wants to spend a lot of time with her girlfriends. Girls' nights out, candle parties, home-decorating parties (how are these different from candle parties, anyway?), cookie exchanges, baby showers, bridal showers. There is always something. You never realized when you were dating what a big part other women played in your wife's life. Is this normal? Should you feel threatened? Why does your wife want to spend so much time with her girlfriends?

answer

▼

Your wife likes to spend time with her girlfriends simply because she enjoys being with her own kind, so to speak. Contrary to what psychologists once told us, men and women are not alike. They don't look alike, they don't think alike, and their emotional makeup isn't alike. Girl time gives your wife a chance to enjoy being herself with people who share the same interests.

You and your wife share interests, and of course she loves to be with you, but the time she spends with her girl-friends allows her to express and share her feminine interests and concerns in a different way than she can with you. This is not only good for her, but it is good for you, too. Think about it. How much do you enjoy going clothes shopping with her, sitting on that dreaded chair outside the dressing room, holding her purse? How much do you want to hear about the flowers for her sister's wedding? Do you really want to help her weigh the pros and cons of one hairdresser over another? Probably no more than she wants to talk about the trouble you had with that project car you're working on. Those times she spends with her girlfriends are part of her well-rounded life, and when you encourage her to enjoy her friendships, you are telling her you love her enough to let her enjoy being a woman.

worth thinking about

▶ **Be supportive** when she says she wants to do something with her friends. Allow her to enjoy her girl time guilt-free.

▶ **Be careful** not to bad-mouth her friends. Your wife has great taste in people (after all, she picked you), so she obviously sees something good in the women she is enjoying. Look again, and you may see it, too.

▶ **If you feel** she's spending more time with her friends than with you, you might offer to spend time in her world. Take her to a movie she's wanted to see. You may actually enjoy it.

> *Friends are the sunshine of life.*
> John Hay

64 question

How can you learn to appreciate her "shopping gene"?

You may have wondered after you got married how one woman could spend so much. Perhaps it was a shock the first time you went shopping together for things for the house. You started out with a wallet full of money and came home with a trunk full of stuff. Your wife seems to have a built-in shopping gene. Is there a way to remove it? Or is there a reason to appreciate it?

answer

Your wife's shopping gene is there for life. And the good news is, as the years go by, you will come to appreciate it. Women love to shop, it's true. But a woman usually shops for a purpose, and that purpose is to beautify and improve her family's life. Some of those things that women buy are small household tools that get incorporated into the running of the home. You don't see them, much as you don't see the rotor in your motor under the car hood, but like that rotor they help make the home run. Kitchen gadgets and tools help her keep your stomach full of good food and your house full of good smells. Home decor items blend together much like the flowers in the garden to create a welcome, homey feel. And then there is the garden itself. A garden is a money-hungry thing, but it is all paint for the canvas of a beautiful home. Sheets, pillowcases, towels, clothes for the kids— there are always needs in a home, which means there will always be a shopping list.

You would probably get tired of the seemingly endless shopping needs. Not your wife. She is a shopping soldier, down in the trenches keeping track of what everyone needs and always scouting for bargains. Shopping is a time-consuming chore, and your wife's shopping gene saves you tons of time. Think of the time she saves you and the way she keeps your home humming, all thanks to that little gene. Now that's something to appreciate.

worth thinking about

▶ **Looking for bargains** is the female equivalent of hunting. Show an interest in what she buys, especially when she's been shopping sales and saving money.

▶ **Shop with her** once in a while so you can see how prices are going up. It's easy to disconnect from the everyday cost of living when you're not in the stores seeing the rising prices.

▶ **If you are** concerned that her shopping gene is out of control, sit down together and work out a budget that you both can feel good about.

> *She looks well to the ways of her household, and does not eat the bread of idleness.*
> Proverbs 31:27, NRSV

question
▼

To what extent do you have to share her with others?

You could happily hop on a Harley and ride off into the sunset with your wife, just the two of you against the world. But she would as soon attach a sidecar and haul along her mother, her sister, her coworkers, her best friend, and maybe even a couple of neighbors. You love her friendly spirit and warm heart, and so does everyone else. But sometimes you simply hate to share. How much do you have to share her with the other people in your lives?

answer
▼

The answer to this question is, as much as she needs and probably more than you want. Most men function fine with few people in their lives. Many a man would be happy living in a mountain cabin with only his woman for company. Many a woman, when offered that kind of a future, would run screaming into the night. Relationships are vital to women. You are the center of your wife's life. You are her love and the man at the center of her heart. But her heart has room for other people, too. So does her life. And so does yours. You need to come first, but when you allow room in back of you for other people, you allow her to be herself. By all means, stake out top-priority times for the two of you to be together, but then let go of those less-important days, those hours of the day when you can be busy doing other things and don't really need her by your side. When you share her with other people, when you hold her loosely enough that she can open her arms to others, you give yourself a contented and secure wife. But there are side benefits. Your wife gains friendship and support for you that will prove invaluable when you find yourselves in need of help. So free her to enjoy the other people in her life, and she will bring good things back to you.

worth thinking about

▶ It will be easier for you to share if you have staked out together time. Make sure you have special days and weekends marked on the calendar for just the two of you.

▶ Sharing is nobler when you do it with a smile. Don't grumble when your wife wants to be social. You may guilt her into giving up time with others that way, but her cooperation won't be cheerful.

▶ See the new people your wife brings into your life as potential friends and allies for you, too. Then you won't be tempted to feel jealous or resentful.

> *Life is fortified by many friendships.*
> Sydney Smith

Do you really have to get into the things she is into?

Sharing and treasuring each other's interests is important to joyful companionship.

Benjamin Devey

question

How can you prove that her interests are a priority to you?

You have interests of your own that you want to pursue, but you understand that marriage is a two-person life-style and that it isn't all about you. Your wife's interests are also important to you, even the ones you don't share, because her happiness is important to you. How can you, as her husband, prove to her that her interests are a priority with you, that what matters to her matters to you as well?

answer

There are many ways you can show your wife that her interests are a priority to you. One is by encouraging her to pursue those interests. This benefits both of you. Her hobbies keep your wife excited about her world and give her something to talk about beyond the business of running the house or the stress at the office. They also help keep your conversations interesting. You can encourage her interests by building time for them into your family schedule and budget.

Even when you can't share an interest, you can still find things about it to appreciate. Needlepoint probably isn't your thing, but you can admire the good job your wife does on hers. You can also find ways to be supportive. If she asks you to stop and pick up spring bulbs at the nursery on your way to the auto-supply shop, your willingness to do so will show her that you are happy to oblige her even though you'll probably never stop to smell the flowers. You may have no desire to try that new French restaurant in town, but when you go because she is dying to try it, you show her that her interests carry weight with you. The language of love allows you to be inconvenienced if something makes her happy and to be open to trying new things for her sake. The language of love says, "If it is important to you, it is important to me." And that's a good language for any husband to speak.

worth thinking about

▶ Leave money in the budget for her to pursue her hobbies. This is one of the biggest ways you can demonstrate your support.

▶ Much of what she enjoys won't be your thing, but don't belittle her interests even if they seem silly or useless to you. If something is important to her, it is important.

▶ Leave room in your family schedules and vacations for what she likes to do. This shows her she isn't just along for the ride. She is important.

> *Don't look out only for your own interests,*
> *but take an interest in others, too.*
> Philippians 2:4, NLT

67

question

Does your favorite chair really have to go?

A home should be comfortable, and there is nothing more comfortable than that old chair you've had since you were in college. You've watched football games in that chair, studied in that chair, played video games in that chair, even thought great thoughts in that chair. It took you a long time to break it in, and it is just the way you like it. Does it really have to go? Shouldn't a husband have some say in how his home is decorated?

answer

The answer to this question is simple, but not easy: yes, your chair has to go, at least to the basement. Your wife wants your home to be comfortable, but she wants it to look nice, too. Men will often choose comfort over aesthetics (which is why they like well-used furniture). Women, however, value beauty, and practicality often takes a backseat to that (which should explain the mystery of why your wife chooses shoes that hurt her feet). So while that hundred-year-old couch may have lots of life left in it or your favorite chair might be the best seat in the house, neither will be her first choice for making your home look loving and inviting.

Even though you are the head of the home, it is your wife who makes it what it is, and that makes home decor her department. She is in large part the one responsible for the home's atmosphere, the way it looks and smells. She wants it to be a thing of beauty, a place where all who enter will smile and feel good. And when something mars that beauty, it ruins the whole effect. Yes, practically speaking, she may want to pitch some pieces of furniture before their time. But that is because your home is her masterpiece. So try not to think that you're losing a chair. Instead, figure that you are gaining a work of art. You can title it *Home, Sweet Husband.*

worth thinking about

▶ Give your old furniture to Goodwill or some other charitable organization, and give it a second life. This will make it less hard to part with.

▶ Stake out a guy space somewhere in the house or garage where you can enjoy all the things you can't part with. As long as it's not in a highly trafficked area, your wife will probably be fine with it.

▶ Give your input when you are picking paint or furniture, but let her have the final say. This kind of thing is important to her.

> *Compromise, if not the spice of life, is its solidity. It's what makes nations great and marriages happy.*
> Phyllis McGinley

68 question

How can you show that you value your wife's concerns?

The things that concern you are often very different from the things that concern your wife. In fact, sometimes you look at what she worries about and find yourself wondering why she's wasting mental and emotional energy on it. But just because you don't understand doesn't mean you don't care. It matters to you that you help her with her concerns because she matters to you. How can you as a husband make sure she knows this?

answer

The first and foremost way you can show her you value her concerns is to give them credence. She has reasons for those concerns. You may not see the big deal in knowing what the dress code is for the office party, but here's why she does: she doesn't want to wear the wrong thing and spend the evening feeling as if she's wearing a sign that reads "Clueless." You may not get why she worries about the baby after you've left Junior with that new babysitter, but she knows disaster can strike in a heartbeat. The new babysitter is a real concern to her because a problem is a very real possibility. So listen. Don't dismiss her concerns or laugh them off. She'll appreciate it if you allow her freedom to express them.

You can also show how much you value her concerns after she voices them by taking whatever action is appropriate and necessary. The last thing you might want to do on a date or a romantic evening is stop and call home to see how Grandma and Grandpa are faring with the kids, but if you cooperate, your wife will feel better and you both will be able to enjoy yourselves more. You may not want to turn back after you're a mile from home because she forgot something, but do it anyway. By behaving as if you value her concerns, you'll never have to reassure her that you do.

worth thinking about

▶ **Acquiesce without** grumbling. Your wife will feel more comfortable to share what's bothering her when she's assured of your acceptance and support.

▶ **Avoid labeling** her concerns as silly, especially when what you probably mean to say is that they are incomprehensible.

▶ **Head off** some problems at the pass by helping her double-check herself. If she tends to worry that she's left the stove on or the iron plugged in when you take a trip, double-check it so you can reassure her. An ounce of prevention is worth a pound of irritation later.

Men are to show a protective and nurturing concern for women that equals (or surpasses) their instinctive concern for their own bodies.
Richard D. Phillips

question

How can you appreciate those woman things you don't understand?

Your wife expects you to adore that cute little home decoration in the store window. "Isn't that cute?" she coos, and you think, *Um*. Sometimes she expects you to rave over a strange dish she's concocted with food combinations no man in his right mind would want to eat. It's times like this you wish there was some sort of training program a husband could take: Woman Stuff Appreciation 101. How can you learn to appreciate the things she wants you to?

answer

The good news is, you don't have to love everything she loves. You can't. If you did, you'd be a woman. Some things you think of as only female-friendly, like certain foods, certain books, certain interests, may be more male-friendly than you realize. Maybe sometimes what's stopping you from appreciating those interests is that you're a little worried what the guys at the office would think. Don't worry about them. You're not married to them.

Be open to trying what she likes and wants to share with you. You may develop a taste for it. Or you may at least develop an appreciation for what's behind it. Even if you never share exactly the same taste in food, you can envision your wife happily chopping, stirring, and seasoning to create that unusual dish and make something new and interesting for you.

As a husband, your best choice is not to look so much at what thrills your wife as to look at why it does and respect that. Those fresh flowers are lovely, they smell good, and they make her house look pretty. That's why she likes them. Even if they don't do it for you, you can probably understand the joy of looking at something nice. Your wife appreciates beauty. You appreciate beauty, too. Yippee for cut flowers! Start looking below the surface at what zings her, and you, too, might actually experience a zing or two.

worth thinking about

▶ **Be open** to trying new things. Some of those things your wife enjoys are really gender-neutral. It's only the culture that labels them male or female.

▶ **Never belittle** or make fun of what thrills her. It may seem silly to you, but it is important to her.

▶ **Even when you** can't understand the thrill of something she likes, make it available to her and enjoy her reaction. Those fresh flowers are always a good place to start.

> *Every good relationship, especially marriage, is based on respect. If it's not based on respect, nothing that appears to be good will last very long.*
>
> Amy Grant

70

question

Is there any way out of taking dancing lessons?

Oh, the things your wife dreams up for you to do together! This, she assures you, will be great fun. Just her, you, and your two left feet. While you have no objections to spending an evening holding your wife in your arms, you're not wild about making a fool of yourself in front of a bunch of strangers. Why does this sort of thing appeal to her? And can you get out of it if it doesn't appeal to you?

answer

Of course you can get out of it. But maybe after hearing why it's important to your wife, you may not want to. Women love to dance. It starts when they're little girls, twirling in their party dresses and enjoying the thrill of watching the skirt swirl around them, and it grows on from there. Girls dance at slumber parties; they dance around in the car seat when a fun song comes on the radio; they sway back and forth while singing lullabies to their babies. For most women, music and movement simply go together. That's the first reason why your wife wants to take dance lessons. The second reason is that it's romantic and thrilling. There is something about being thrown around by a sexy man (that's you) that simply makes her buzz. The look of love in your eyes, your strong arms around her, the music, that new dress she bought—they all add up to a great evening for her.

What's the good news for you if you give in, get your dancing shoes, and go trip the light fantastic? The dance floor is a place where men are men and women must follow wherever they lead. You get to decide every move she makes. You get to enjoy your masculinity to the hilt. And the more you take charge, the more she'll like it. You'll literally dance your way deeper into her heart. That should be worth enduring a little embarrassment over those two left feet.

worth thinking about

▶ **Sign up** for a few lessons on a trial basis, maybe through your local parks department. If you are challenged in the areas of rhythm and grace, ask the dance instructor which dance is the easiest to learn and start with that.

▶ **Make a deal.** If you take dance lessons, maybe your wife will try something you want to do. Your willingness to waltz that extra mile may inspire her to try rock climbing or camping.

▶ **If your wife** has been longing to take dancing lessons, surprise her with some for Valentine's Day, Christmas, or her birthday.

> *Dancing is good for your heart,*
> *both physically and romantically.*
> Bob Stritof

question

▼

Why do the children sometimes seem to come first?

Way back when it was just you and her, you were your wife's everything, her number one priority. And then the kids came along, and you detected a shift in your relationship. You know in your head that you're still the love of her life, but you're not always number one. How is it that you sometimes feel you have to wait in line behind the children for her attention? As her husband and head of the house, aren't you supposed to come first?

answer

▼

Yes, you should come first. And you do, in her heart. But she also has a responsibility to take care of those little ones who can't always take care of themselves. There may be nothing your wife would like better at the end of a long, busy day than to sit down and relax with you when you come in the door. If she has a fussy baby on her hip and is trying to make dinner for the rest of the gang, she may not be able to oblige, not unless your preschoolers are kitchen prodigies. Raising children to be responsible adults is a huge obligation, and the great work of her life. A child who is sick, in trouble, or in need of counseling is going to take precedence over adult needs. Your wife will assume that you, being big and strong, can survive just fine without her attention for a while, but that child, small and vulnerable, can't.

Mothers seem hardwired to protect and care for their young. You wouldn't want your wife to be any other way because you, too, care for your children, and you want them to turn out happy and well adjusted. Allowing your wife to be the dedicated mother she is called to be may bring some irritation during those child-rearing years, but if you can sacrifice along with her, you will both reap the benefit of having a great relationship with good kids.

worth thinking about

▶ **When you have** a sick child, take a turn with the nursing care so your wife can get some rest. She can't meet either the child's needs or yours when she's exhausted.

▶ **Give the children** tons of attention when they're awake, but then put them to bed early enough so that you and your wife can enjoy adult time together.

▶ **If you feel** that your wife is neglecting you for the children and that you're growing apart, ask her on a date. Putting time for the two of you on the calendar will help it rate a higher priority.

> *A Christian mother is the greatest heritage God can give a man.*
> Author Unknown

question
▼
Why do you have to hang that picture right now?

Chores like picture hanging rarely make it to the top of your priority list. Whether you're moving into a new house or simply maintaining the old one, you have tons of things to do. The last thing you want is to abandon getting the garage squared away so that you can hold up a picture in six different locations for your wife to see where it looks best. Does she really need your assistance to put holes in the wall? Can you put this off?

answer
▼

For your wife, the house doesn't feel like home unless it has pictures on the walls. She probably doesn't expect you to drop an important project to be at her beck and call, but she does want you to take an interest in her efforts to make your home look nice. Some of those efforts require two sets of hands. Picture hanging is definitely a two-person job. It is also a lot like trimming the Christmas tree, and all those other homey chores that women place a high priority on—it's more fun when it is done by two people.

For a woman, having to do this kind of thing by herself makes her feel alone, as if she's the only one who cares about your marriage and your home life. You know that's not true. For you, it's simply a matter of priorities and preferences. Some things simply aren't as important to you. Some of those household chores you could happily live without ever doing because you wouldn't miss them if they were gone. For instance,you wouldn't mourn the loss of searching through books of designer wallpaper, mixing just the right shade of green or yellow or blue, or coordinating fabric stripes and florals. But your wife would, and that's why it's a good thing to set aside the book you're reading or the putt you're practicing in order to hang the picture. When you join her in this kind of little project, you tell her that yes, this is your home, too, and you love it as much as she does. And even more important, you love her.

worth thinking about

▶ When helping your wife with domestic chores you don't particularly care about, remember that you don't particularly care, and let her make the final decisions. Don't micromanage her.

▶ Resist the temptation to urge her to "hurry up and make a decision" so you can get back to what you were doing.

▶ Your wife will thank you for your help. Take a moment after the job is done to admire how it turned out and tell her you appreciate her.

> *Great opportunities to help others seldom come, but small ones surround us every day.*
> Sally Koch

73

What's the best gift you can give her on holidays?

You love to see your wife's eyes light up when you give her something great. That is an experience well worth repeating. Sometimes she doesn't get quite so excited, and that can get discouraging. You want everything you give her to be the kind of present that makes her throw her arms around you. Is there a type of holiday present that comes with a wife-satisfaction guarantee? What is a sure way to make your wife happy at the holidays?

answer

What your wife treasures most about the gifts you give her has nothing to do with how cool they are or what you've spent on them. Well, all right, she'll probably get pretty excited if you give her those diamond earrings she's been eyeing. Most women love jewelry. But all women love a present that shows how much their man thought about them when he was selecting it. That whole selection thing can feel daunting. What if she doesn't like it? This is why some men chicken out and give their wives money. On the surface, that's nice. No sweat. Problem solved. But a wife can look at this kind of present and think that you didn't put any thought into it and actually feel hurt. You are better off not to think in terms of what to buy for her. Think instead in terms of what to give her.

She wants something that says you thought long and hard before picking this one special thing because you knew she'd love it. And that means you have to really pay attention to her interests, to what she raves over, yearns for, or asks of you personally. Whether a present is something you buy, something you make, or something special you do, remember that your wife is not interested in how much you spend. She's interested in how much you care.

worth thinking about

▶ **The more thought** you put into a present, the more valuable it will be to your wife. Make her a coupon book full of coupons good for things she loves: back rubs, breakfast in bed, etc.

▶ **Try getting** something sentimental framed, like a certificate or diploma she's earned or a picture of the two of you taken on some special occasion.

▶ **Your perfect present** to her may be a promise to spend more time together in the coming year or to work on kicking a bad habit she's been begging you to break. Don't be afraid to think outside the box.

> *May no gift be too small to give nor to simple to receive, which is wrapped in thoughtfulness, and tied up in love.*
> L. O. Baird

74

What do love and good listening skills have in common?

Most of the time you're interested in what your wife has to say, but sometimes she wants to talk more than your ears are able to listen. Or she talks about things you can't identify with, and your mind wanders. She can tell when you have tuned her out and are just pretending to listen. Those are the times she begins to compare true love to listening skills. Surely there can't be a link. Can there?

answer

There may not be a link in your mind, but there is in your wife's. You are the man to whom she gave her heart. That means she also made you the man she turns to when she has problems or concerns and wants to talk. Granted, she probably often wants to talk about things that seem to be of no consequence, and those are the times you may be tempted to tune out. But anything your wife desires to discuss is of consequence to her, so for a loving husband, tuning out really isn't an option. You're telling her something when you don't listen. You're announcing that you are not interested in what she has to say, and to her that translates into "Your feelings don't matter."

When you listen to what your wife says, she feels valued. She is reassured that her thoughts and feelings are important to you. The more you listen, the more she will trust you and the more secure she will feel. Being a good listener brings so many other benefits. Because your wife feels she can tell you anything, she will. And the more she confides in you, the more she trusts you. The more she trusts you, the closer you two become. And the closer you become, the more you can trust her as well. Good teamwork consists of good communication. Your listening ear will prove your love and make the two of you a winning team.

worth thinking about

▶ An important part of good listening involves believing what you hear. Always assume when your wife is talking to you that she is being truthful.

▶ Listening takes time, so when you give your wife time and attention, you show her how much you value her.

▶ If you feel that things haven't been going well between you and your wife, check to see how much you've been communicating lately. A lack of listening could be part of the problem.

> *The first duty of love is to listen.*
> Paul Tillich

question

How can you be a good listener?

If listening is an important way to show your wife you love her, then you want to be a good listener. This woman is your other half, your soul mate, and you want to make sure she knows that when she talks, she has your ear. Listening, like so much of what you do, is a skill. How can you develop that skill? How can you be a good listener? Are there some specific how-to's you should know about?

answer

Good listening means paying attention. You listen not only with your ears, but with your mind and heart as well. You need to have your mind involved because sometimes you'll need to translate what your wife is saying. Sweeping generalizations often have an underlying meaning. Statements that begin with "We never" or "You never" really mean "I want." So if your wife says, "We never do anything fun," she really means, "I want to go out together." You may wonder why, if that is what she means, she never comes right out and says it. Perhaps she doesn't say what she wants because she fears you won't hear. So she skips Step One and goes right to Step Two, putting her request in stronger language, hoping a little guilt will achieve the desired results.

The better you get at listening, the less she'll feel the need to resort to those sweeping generalizations. You not only need your mind fully engaged when talking with your wife, you want your emotions involved as well. Often when she speaks, your wife is looking for concern and empathy. If she is telling you about the hard day she had, she will be looking for clues that you really heard, like comforting words and body language. When she tells you something she feels strongly about, she looks to see that emotion mirrored in your eyes as well. Fully engage and respond when she talks, and you will have mastered the most important good listening skill.

worth thinking about

▶ **Keep eye contact** when your wife is talking. If she has to compete with the TV or newspaper, she will doubt that you are really paying attention.

▶ **Ask questions.** An engaged listener responds verbally to the person who is talking to him.

▶ **When she wants** to talk, welcome her with a smile so she won't feel that she is inconveniencing you. If you are in the middle of something, promise to give her your undivided attention as soon as you are done.

> *If a husband can overlook the actual words his wife uses to express herself and instead actively pursue what she means, fewer arguments will take place.*
> Gary Smalley

Why is it important to be a good listener?

We often tell couples that almost all of their conflicting conversations could be resolved if each partner would seek to understand before being understood—in other words, if each would learn to listen.

Leslie and Les Parrott

76 question

What's the best proof that you have heard your wife?

Sometimes you find it hard to believe that your wife would question whether or not you were listening to her. Why would you ignore someone who is so important to you? You love her and want to make her happy. It bothers you when she suggests that you weren't listening. Is there something you as a husband can do to prevent this kind of misunderstanding? How can you prove that you listen to what she has to say?

answer

Responding when your wife speaks is the best proof that you have heard her. This doesn't mean you agree with what she's saying or agree to what she wants. But it does mean you actively acknowledge that she's telling you something and you are interested in her opinions and care about her concerns. When she says that blue is her favorite color and you buy her a blue sweater for her birthday, you show not only that you were paying attention when she spoke but also that what she said was important. When you ask her later in the day how that meeting she was worried about went, she knows you heard, not only about the meeting, but about her concerns. It speaks volumes about your listening skills when you work on solving a problem she has brought up or when you take a step toward tackling something difficult that you are facing as a couple.

Anyone can hear, but not everyone can listen. Listening does something. It produces emotion, reaction, and results. You can say you've heard your wife, but when you behave as if you have, you will prove it. She will not only be grateful for this, she will listen to and cooperate with you as well. This can produce a cycle of loving behavior that can only serve to make your marriage stronger. So show her you are listening by the way you respond, and you will both benefit.

worth thinking about

- ▶ **When your wife** asks for changes from you that will benefit you and the family, take note and make them.

- ▶ **Pay attention** when she talks about her schedule. If she has a doctor's appointment, your asking later how it went will show you were listening.

- ▶ **Listen when she's** wishing. It's not always practical or doable to give your wife her heart's desire, but when you can, go for it, especially if it's something sentimental and related to the family. It will thrill her to know you have your ear tuned to hear her heart's desire.

> *Actions are more significant than words.*
> Gersham Bulkeley

77

question
▼
Why should you listen to your wife's advice?

You don't remember your wife's being so full of advice when you were dating. She thought you could do no wrong. But now that you are married, she seems to think you could use a little help on a lot of things. You do a pretty good job as the guy in charge. So why does your wife seem to think you need advice? And do you really need to take it? Doesn't that make you less of a man, less of a husband?

answer
▼

As a man, you want your wife to have confidence in your abilities and to trust your judgment. When she offers advice, you feel as if she doesn't think you measure up. But that's not the case. Your wife doesn't give advice because she wants to tear you down; she gives it because she wants to help you. Being a woman, she is big into teamwork, and giving advice is often her way of showing you she is part of the team.

Sometimes a wife can see things a husband can't, especially when it comes to relationships. A man may say something to a friend or family member and never realize it was hurtful. His wife, who has been picking up signals since she was six, can read the situation and see what has happened. Not wanting a problem to grow, she will tell her husband, "You hurt Joe's feelings. You'd better make it right." By pointing out a problem, his wife has helped him avert a relationship problem.

God put your wife by your side to be your friend and companion. God put her by your side to help you. She comes to you equipped with unique insights and a different way of thinking, and that gives you twice the brainpower to use when coping with life's challenges. Next time she offers advice, listen to it, and then consider it with an open mind. You could truly find it helpful.

worth thinking about

▶ **If your wife** tends to give advice in an abrasive manner, discuss her method of delivery. Suggest she use a more diplomatic phrase like "You might want to," and explain that this will make you more open to taking her advice.

▶ **Remember** that your wife is offering help because she cares about you, so when she does, don't take it as an insult.

▶ **Whether or not** you take her advice, thank her for caring enough to give it. By doing this, you'll avoid shutting her down—and you won't wind up needing advice on how to get out of the doghouse.

> *A capable wife who can find? She is far more precious than jewels. The heart of her husband trusts in her, and he will have no lack of gain. She does him good, and not harm, all the days of her life.*
>
> Proverbs 31:10–12, NRSV

question

How do you translate female-speak?

Sometimes, even though you are sure you have been listening carefully to what your wife said, you still wind up misunderstanding her. It's as if she is speaking a foreign language. You see her lips moving, you hear words coming out of her mouth, words that are familiar even, but for her they can have an entirely different meaning than they do for you. How can you, as a husband, learn to translate female-speak?

answer

What your wife says can sometimes seem like a foreign language. Certain words and phrases often take on whole new meanings when your wife is using them. But is that really so surprising? Different families and different lifestyles can charge the same word with different meanings, and when you add gender differences to the mix, a man can often feel the need for a dictionary. You may have noticed that your wife doesn't always define *fun* the way you do. Or *help*. Or *cute*. Or even *love*. So when she suggests that something would be fun for the two of you to do, something that you perceive as torture, stop and think about her reference point. Is this something her family always enjoyed? Is this something women generally enjoy? If the answer to either of those questions is yes, then there's your definition.

When she makes vague statements like "I think we have a problem," translation can be a little harder. Your thoughts spin a hundred directions. *We have a problem at home? Where? What kind of problem?* Understand that when your wife makes a statement that seems vague to you, she assumes that because you are close you must be tuned in to her thoughts and concerns. She is tuned in to yours. Even with hard work, you may never completely understand female-speak. But always remember that whatever language she is speaking, your wife loves you.

worth thinking about

▶ **When your wife** says something and you are uncertain what she means, ask for clarification. Explain that you want to understand, but you're not getting what she is trying to tell you.

▶ **When discussing** important issues, pick a location where you won't be interrupted and make sure you have allowed enough time for the two of you to communicate clearly. No matter what you say, always make sure you say it with love.

▶ **Studying any foreign** language takes time. Don't give up on understanding your wife's.

> *Everyone has his or her own definition for a given word.*
> Gary Smalley

79

question

▼

What is your wife saying when she doesn't speak?

When your wife is angry and speaking, you at least have a hope of figuring out what is bothering her, but when she turns silent you have a problem. You know you're in trouble because she may turn her back on you or go into another room. You may catch her wiping at her eyes, a sure sign that she is hiding tears. Why doesn't she come right out and say what is bothering her? What is the message behind the silent treatment?

answer

▼

If there is a problem and a wife stops talking, it is not because she has figured, "Oh, well. I love him anyway. I'll let this go." When she turns silent, here is what she is saying: "I am so hurt and angry right now, I cannot even put what I'm feeling into words. If I tell you what I'm thinking, it will be really ugly. Anyway, I have so many angry thoughts rolling around in my head, I hardly know where to start." There's the first half of what she's saying. Often there is a whole second message following close behind: "I dare you to ask me what I'm thinking. Just go ahead and try. Then I'll really let you have it." Now, aren't you glad you asked?

The good news is, your wife doesn't want to stay in this condition. She wants to heal the hurt, restore the normal good relationship you share, and return to closeness. So hear what she is saying. Even when you're not anxious to get an answer, ask her to tell you what's wrong or, if you know what is wrong, tell her you're sorry. When a woman is hurt, allowing her to stay behind that wall of silence will do neither of you any good. Woo her out from behind it and keep listening when she speaks.

worth thinking about

▶ **If you ask** your wife what's wrong and she says, "Nothing," it never means "Nothing." More likely it means, "I don't think I can work up the nerve to tell you and deal with the consequences." Don't take that initial refusal to open up as license to give up and leave her alone. Stay determined to fix the problem.

▶ **When trying** to get to the bottom of her silence, use a concerned tone of voice and a gentle touch.

▶ **Be prepared** to devote however much time is needed to learning what is bothering her and to helping her feel better.

> *After counseling numerous troubled marriages, I have observed that distressed marriages frequently are weak in the domain of repentance and short on apologies.*
> Randall A. Schroeder

question

How can you know what she's really angry about?

There may have been times when you thought you and your wife were arguing over one thing, but you eventually learned that you were really fighting over something entirely different. You want to solve every problem that may arise between you, but first you have to actually know what the problem is. And sometimes you don't. In fact, sometimes you're not sure she even does. If your wife is angry, how can you get to the root of what is bothering her?

answer

A wife is a little like a computer, only with emotions. She gathers information and stores it in her memory bank. When she is angry you may simply be seeing the last saved document. There could be several offenses filed in the back of her mind that led up to this moment. Perhaps you have splashed water all over the bathroom, leaving it looking like a baby whale stopped by for a swim. She may fume over this, but what has really aggravated her is the backlog of bathroom messes and the problems lying behind them, which she perceives as a lack of consideration for her and a cavalier attitude toward your home.

If leaving a disaster in your wake is a habit, know that she's not really angry over this one mess you're quarreling about; she's angry over all the messes. If you are discussing an overdrawn checkbook, and she explodes or bursts into tears, it probably has less to do with the checkbook and more to do with her frustration that there isn't enough money in the bank to pay all the bills.

It is always good to look carefully to see if there have been similar incidents leading up to the one currently causing a problem. Is there a deeper root from which your wife's anger has sprung? Like any good detective, if you backtrack and follow the clues, you will get to the bottom of what is really making her angry.

worth thinking about

▶ **Put yourself** in her shoes and look at a situation from her eyes. You might be surprised how quickly you figure out what is really bothering her.

▶ **Come right out** and ask her what is bothering her. But when you do, make sure you are not asking using a defensive tone of voice and body language. Outstretched hands and a perturbed "What?" won't exactly make her want to tell you why she's upset.

▶ **Don't ask** until you are prepared to hear the answer.

> *Most people spend more time and energy going around problems than in trying to solve them.*
> Henry Ford

81

question

Is everything okay if you are not fighting?

When you have gone through a stormy period, it can feel like a relief when the fighting stops. No raised voices, no hurt looks, no disagreements. You have had the last word, and everything is settled. Your wife has come around. Peace at last. But is this the kind of peace where you can sigh happily and sink back in your recliner, or is it the calm before the storm? Is it really all quiet on the home front when your wife is keeping silent?

answer

Silence is not always golden, at least not in marriage. A husband can hope all is well when his wife stops arguing, but if he is tuned in, he usually knows deep down when things are no longer right between him and his beloved. A wife can give up the verbal tug of war, let go of the rope, and walk away, but if she leaves feeling unheard or uncared for, she will leave hurt. She'll stop talking because she figures it is futile, that he's not going to listen anyway. Her husband can deceive himself for a time into thinking this is peace, because what man likes to argue with his wife? But that deception gets uncomfortable quickly. No man wants to feel that he won the war but lost the battle, that he made his point but lost her respect.

There may be times when you and your wife find yourselves strongly in disagreement and you end the disagreement with more force than grace. Or perhaps you pressure her into going along with something she's not comfortable with. She may stop fighting you, but if you haven't come to an amicable compromise or ended your disagreement with a hug and a kiss, you can be sure this is not the silence of a contented woman. Don't drift along like a leaf on the river. Open the lines of communication and talk to your wife until you are both functioning as one again. That way, you'll never see the rapids.

worth thinking about

▶ **When your wife** grows silent, check her body language. Has she stopped smiling? Stopped looking at you? Did she stiffen when you put your arm around her? These are big clues that you need to lovingly reconnect.

▶ **If she keeps** to a different portion of the house when you are both home, make sure she's not avoiding you. Avoidance is a deadly silence that slices a chasm between husband and wife. Bridge it quickly before it can grow.

▶ **When you've had** to make a difficult decision that has been hard for her, check periodically to see how she's doing.

> *A wife simply will not respond to her husband when he continually hurts her feelings without "clearing the slate"—draining away her anger.*
> Gary Smalley

question

▼

Why should you listen to what she says to others?

You've probably heard the expression "Talk is cheap." But sometimes talk can be valuable, especially when that talk tells what is in the heart. And as a loving husband, you want to always know what is in your wife's heart. Is there something to be learned when you and your wife are out together and she is talking with other people or when you are within listening range when she's talking with her friends? If so, what?

answer

▼

Sometimes the best way to take the temperature of your relationship is to observe what your wife reveals to other people. This doesn't mean you should hide around corners and eavesdrop, but when you are nearby, pay attention. Women use talking to vent, especially when they are with other women. If your wife is frustrated over something going on between the two of you, chances are she'll commiserate about it with her girlfriends. While you and the guys are gathered around the punch bowl talking about the game, she and the other wives are probably in the kitchen discussing all of you. A woman doesn't see this as a betrayal of her husband. She simply sees it as a chance to share with her friends and either brag or get sympathy.

She will brag about you as quickly as she'll lament. If you have gone the extra mile, said something sweet, given her an unexpected present, or been there for her during a difficult time, she will most likely announce it everywhere you go. It's a great feeling to get those public brags, but if you overhear a complaint, pay attention. It could mean she thinks you are not listening at home, and she is resorting to the use of a public forum to get your attention. Always remember, you can hide your true self from many people, but not your wife, and if you want to hear good of yourself in public, make it your policy to do good in private.

worth thinking about

▶ **If your wife** says something when you are out together that you think is inappropriate, don't add gasoline to the fire by responding then and there. Talk about it when the two of you are alone.

▶ **It's hard to** get taken by surprise in a public setting, so encourage your wife to tell you first when she's unhappy with you. That way, if she lets something slip when you're out together, you at least won't be caught off guard.

▶ **Thank her** when she says something nice about you in public, and tell her how good it makes you feel.

> *Your reputation is what people say about you; your character is what God and your wife know about you.*
> Billy Sunday

83 question

What's the perfect response when your wife's not perfect?

Your wife is close to perfect. Still, there are times when, great as she is, she can act less than perfect. Some of the little flaws you found so endearing in her when you first met, are the same flaws that can frustrate you now that you're married. You can find yourself frustrated, irritated, or even downright angry. But you don't want your response to become part of the problem. How can you respond to your wife when you are angry with her?

answer

The perfect response is to control your anger. You are allowed to feel it. Emotions are part of being human. But whether you are simply irritated or ready to put your fist through a wall, you have to harness that emotion and make it behave in a civilized manner. This means you cannot fly into a rage. An out-of-control male temper is terrifying to a woman, and a rampaging husband will make her want to run away. (Not an effective method for resolving differences.)

You can get a handle on your anger more quickly if you take a moment to remind yourself of some very important facts. This is the woman you chose; this is the woman you love. And she is married to a man who is no more perfect than she is. Bearing these facts in mind will help you approach your wife with a little more patience. And patience is a good tool for managing anger. Patience forces you to take a deep breath and explain exactly why you are not happy. It helps you cope with her imperfect behavior, and it also helps you work toward making things better between you. Your wife will never be perfect any more than you will be. But if you can work through those times when she's not, you will have a marriage that is happily close to perfect.

worth thinking about

▶ Go to the gym and run on the treadmill when you feel your anger about to take control. You'll burn off some steam and be better able to cope with what is bothering you.

▶ When you argue with your wife, fight fair. Tell her specifically what she's doing that is bugging you and why, but never belittle her or resort to name-calling.

▶ Always stand ready to forgive her. Don't hold on to your anger.

> *Don't get so angry that you sin.*
> *Don't go to bed angry.*
> Ephesians 4:26, CEV

84 **question**

Who should you talk to when you're mad at her?

Building a life together is exciting, but it can also be hard work, especially when you and your wife are having trouble working as a team. Even though you try hard to be patient, there are times when you find yourself confused, clueless, and frustrated. You've reached a stalemate, or she's hurt you deeply. You don't know what to do. All you know is that you are mad and have lost your way as a husband. Who can you talk to?

answer

When you feel that you are not getting anywhere resolving a problem with your wife, when you're feeling frustrated or discouraged over problems in your relationship, you definitely need to talk to someone. And the One to go to is God. He understands how you are feeling better than anyone because He made you. And He made your wife. The workings of her mind and heart are no mystery to Him. And your problems are not insurmountable to Him, either. God loves both you and your wife as no one else can, so it only makes sense to turn to Him first. Having made both of you and caring for both of you, He also holds the wisdom you need for whatever you are dealing with. When you are having problems, other people can sympathize, but they may offer advice that is tainted by their own biases and beliefs. By going straight to the Maker Himself, you eliminate that problem.

God is more than willing to give you the wisdom you need to cope with whatever is bothering you. When you talk to Him, you have a safe place to vent. You can say anything. He won't be shocked. When you talk to Him, you plug into the ultimate source of wisdom. Remember Solomon? When he was God's man, he was the wisest man in the world. If you want wisdom, if you want to know you are talking to someone who really cares, God is the counselor for you.

worth thinking about

▶ Spend time every day praying for your marriage and for wisdom as a husband. This will keep you tuned in to God and will keep you spiritually fit to stop problems before they grow big enough to make you angry.

▶ Memorize scripture verses, especially ones that can comfort and guide you when you and your wife are going through a rough patch. Invest in a Bible concordance so you can look up verses that will help you.

▶ When you and your wife are arguing, stop and pray for love, patience, and guidance. This can be a quick way to diffuse anger.

> If you don't know what you're doing, pray to the Father. He loves to help. You'll get his help, and won't be condescended to when you ask for it.
>
> James 1:5, THE MESSAGE

question

▼

How do you get back that loving feeling when you're mad?

You know that love is a behavior, a way of life, and it is more than feelings. Still, it bothers you when you are upset with your wife and you feel angry with her rather than tender toward her. What can you do when she has brought out the worst in you and the last thing you want to feel about her is love? Is there something you can do to get over those negative feelings and bring back the love?

answer

▼

Your feelings are governed by what goes on in your brain. When your wife says or does something thoughtless, your brain says, *Wait a minute. That wasn't cool. Something needs to be done about this.* Those are the marching orders for your feelings to get involved and to manufacture hurt. When she does something you think is inconsiderate, again your brain processes the action, gives it a thumbs-up or a thumbs-down, and your feelings respond accordingly. Once your feelings are off and running, reverse the process to pull them back. You used your brain to direct your feelings to produce some anger pronto; now you need to use your brain to flip the shutoff valve and stop the flow. You can do this by redirecting your thoughts.

Just as you thought about all the reasons why you should be angry, you can also think about all the reasons why you should love your wife anyway. Redirect your focus away from the negative to the positive, and start thinking about all your wife's good qualities and about how important she is to you. Look at what you have built together, and thank God that He has given you the ability to rise above your anger and forgive your wife. When you start thinking kind and generous thoughts, you'll find that your emotions soon get the message and start producing loving feelings again.

worth thinking about

▶ **When you are** having a hard time feeling loving toward your wife, list six things you admire about her.

▶ **Think back** to the most recent close time you enjoyed together. What were you doing? How can you replicate that closeness?

▶ **Take out an old** photo album or look at pictures on disk of the two of you together, enjoying each other. Remember the good times you had in the past, and assure yourself that you will find a way to have more in the future.

> *He that cannot forgive others, breaks the*
> *bridge over which he himself must pass*
> *if he would ever reach heaven; for*
> *everyone has need to be forgiven.*
> George Herbert

What is the most important thing to remember when there are problems?

I have told you all this so that you may have peace in me. Here on earth you will have many trials and sorrows. But take heart, because I have overcome the world.

John 16:33, NLT

question

How can you help your wife stay happy about staying on a budget?

You want your family to be secure financially, and you know that in order for that to happen you have to keep spending from getting out of control. The best way to do that is with a budget. Your wife translates the word *budget* to mean straitjacket, so you have a challenge. How can you convince her that this is a good thing, and how can you help her not only to cooperate, but to do so with enthusiasm?

answer

It's not always fun staying on a budget. In fact, it can be hard work. It can be especially hard when needs arise that you forgot to budget for. Those are the times when your wife may be most tempted to figure it's not working and toss the whole thing. So it is a good idea to keep the troops rallied. For that to happen, you need to keep your family goals in front of her. Redirect her mental gaze to the goal at the end of the budget road, and remind her why you are sacrificing now. Keep her excited about the progress you are making by reminding her how much your family is going to benefit in the long run from her sacrifice in the short term.

Your encouragement and gratitude are key factors that can help your wife stay happy on a budget. When you encourage her to hang in there, you let her know that you believe in her, that you know she can do it. Your gratitude, especially when a tight budget is pinching her, can show her you need and appreciate her help. In an environment of hope and encouragement, a woman can deal with anything. When your wife knows you appreciate her, and she sees that you are working with her to keep your home financially stable and your family well, she can also be happy.

worth thinking about

▶ Track your progress together. This reminds your wife that you are a team.

▶ Appeal to the bargain hunter in her by encouraging her to come in under budget on some household items like clothes or food. If she does, designate the savings as a bonus she can spend on whatever she wants.

▶ Celebrate your financial successes together. Financial expert Dave Ramsey suggests that when trying to get out of debt, you pay off the small bills first. That way you'll have something to celebrate.

> *If married, spouses need to do the budget together.*
> *The preacher said ". . . and you are ONE."*
> Dave Ramsey

question

What do you do when your goals conflict?

While you are a pair, a couple, a team, you and your wife are also individuals with unique talents, hopes, and dreams, not to mention likes, dislikes, temperaments, and viewpoints. Those differences can complement each other, making your life richer. But sometimes they result in opposing goals. And when that happens you have conflict. What should you as a husband do when you find that not only are you and your wife not on the same page, but you're not even reading the same story?

answer

There's a saying popular among fiction writers: "Goals in opposition equals conflict." Writers know that for a hero and a heroine to have a problem, they both need to want something different that will involve sacrifice from the other person. Whether in fiction or real life, this principle holds true. When you and your wife both want things that are mutually exclusive, you have a challenge: one of you must find a way to adjust his or her goals so that you can both pull together on the path to a common goal. Sometimes you can compromise. This is easy when it's a small matter of staying home and watching the game on TV or going to your in-laws'. You can record the game to watch later and go to her family's. But in bigger matters, like whether or not to take that new job and move, it gets hard.

Your job as a husband is to always make sure that pursuing your goal won't make your wife suffer. If it will, you could be thinking selfishly, and you may need to reassess. The same principle holds true when she wants to do something. As a loving wife, she doesn't want to make you miserable. Don't lose heart when faced with big decisions where you both want something very different. You still can find a way to move the same direction. But the key to finding it is to keep talking and praying together until you do.

worth thinking about

▶ **When trying** to resolve conflicting goals, assess how much sacrifice will be involved for your wife, then ask yourself if you feel honorable accepting it.

▶ **Never railroad** your wife into going along with a decision. Neither of you will be happy.

▶ **When you find** that you're at a stalemate, get help. Go to your pastor or an older couple you respect for advice.

> *As a couple, you must be determined and committed to resolving conflict. Resolving conflict requires effort and sometimes even great determination to see it through to the end. The rewards, however, of resolved conflict are worth every bit of effort that you put into that resolution.*
> Steven P. Wickstrom

question

▼

How can you show your love when she's feeling down?

A woman's emotions are a mystery to most men. After all, how can a man be expected to understand someone who cries both when she's happy and when she's sad? And when she is sad or feeling discouraged and he tries to help her fix her troubles, often, instead of the grateful response he expected, his advice is greeted with "You don't understand." Which is true. He doesn't. But that can be fixed, and it's not as hard as you might think.

answer

▼

The best way you can love your wife when she's discouraged and disheartened is by putting your arms around her, letting her cry, and giving her words of empathy and encouragement. When a woman is unhappy, she doesn't want to brainstorm a solution to her problem. She doesn't want a pep talk or a shrink session, either. Instead, she wants to talk about the how's and why's of what she's feeling. You, as a man, naturally want to take action. You want to fix the problem. But she is more concerned with fixing how she feels about the problem. For her that is the first step. If she can pull her feelings together, then she can more easily pull her life together.

Sometimes the cause of her unhappiness isn't anything you can fix anyway. Sometimes she's down simply because her hormones have shifted. Once they re-shift, so will her outlook on life. Meanwhile, a hug and some kind words from you can do a lot to relieve the negative emotional symptoms of a temporary physical condition. Sometimes she's tired, stressed, or discouraged. The best antidote for any of those problems is emotional support from you, her husband. She's looking for comfort and reassurance, and by giving her that, you'll be demonstrating your love in a way she will really appreciate.

worth thinking about

▶ **If your wife** is unhappy, first ask yourself if you're the cause. If you are, an "I'm sorry" will help her start feeling better. If you're not, then give her a listening ear. Offer her the strength of your embrace and your empathy.

▶ **Ask if** there is anything you can do to help her. There may not be, but the fact that you offered will comfort her.

▶ **Soothe her** with encouraging words like "It will be all right," or "We'll get through this." Your strong arms coupled with your words of comfort will be the best balm for her emotional hurts.

> *Anxiety weighs down the human heart,*
> *but a good word cheers it up.*
> Proverbs 12:25, NRSV

question

▼

How can you help when your wife loses her job?

Maybe she comes home in tears, or maybe she calls you at the office. "Honey, I lost my job." You feel for her. You know what a sucker punch it is to hear that your services are no longer required. Your wife is diligent and hardworking, and you can hardly imagine this happening to her. And you have no idea what you can do to make it better. How can you help her cope when this happens?

answer

▼

Reassurance is the best balm you can give your wife, and she needs it regarding many different things. If her paycheck has been a big part of your family budget, she will be worried about how you are going to make up the difference. You know that you have always been fine and that you will be in the future. You have faith that everything will work out and that the two of you will weather this setback. Convey that to your wife, and not only will you help her fight off the worry, but you will also relieve her of guilt over not being able to do her part to help pay the bills. She also needs to know that you will find a way to work things out in spite of this setback. Reassure her that you will be fine and that she can take hope.

There is another area where she may also need help, an issue that you as a man are familiar with. If your wife loved her job, she may have gotten her identity wrapped up in it. With the job gone, she's not sure who she is. How does she redefine her days, her life, herself? How does she answer when someone asks her what she does? Of course your wife is more than her job. She is so many things to so many people. Remind her of that, give her your support, and she will soon find herself again. Maybe she'll even find another job.

worth thinking about

▶ Give her lots of empathy and give her plenty of opportunity to talk about how she feels. The more she can talk about what happened, the better she'll be able to process it.

▶ Don't expect her to bounce back immediately and be her normal happy self. Allow her some time to mourn.

▶ Don't suggest she look for a new job. You may want to help her get proactive, but she will think you're pressuring her. She doesn't like feeling as if she's only a paycheck any more than you do. Give her time to get her emotional feet under her.

> *Put your trust in the God who is above anything life can throw at you. The greater the trial or loss, the greater God's faithfulness.*
> Brent Riggs

90

question

▼

How can you calm her fears when you've lost your job?

You knew it was coming. There was talk about downsizing and cutbacks in personnel. Still, it doesn't make being let go any easier. It's one thing to help your wife when she loses her job, but it's another to keep her from panicking when you lose yours. You can barely keep yourself from panicking. How can you see your way ahead and calm her fears, too? How can you keep her calm and find your way to a new job?

answer

▼

It is scary for a husband to have to come home, face his wife, and say, "Honey, I lost my job." She really has no idea what that costs you, how hard it is to fail, and how much you hate to disappoint her. When a wife receives this kind of news, all she sees is that the main source of her family's income has suddenly dried up. Her first thoughts are *How will we survive? How will we make the mortgage payment?* Those are legitimate questions, ones to which a husband doesn't always have an answer. If your wife asks you these questions and you don't yet have a specific plan, your answer must be, "I don't know how yet, but we will get through this."

There will come a time, after she's had a chance to process what is happening, that your wife will come alongside you, support you emotionally, and pitch in to take up the financial slack. But first she must be emotionally armed for battle. And that is where you come in, even though you yourself feel like the walking wounded. Remind her that you have not starved in the past and that you won't in the future. God has not abandoned you. You will get through this together. These are good words for your wife to hear. They will encourage her. And they will encourage you, too.

worth thinking about

▶ Explain any severance package you will be receiving, and lay out any other immediate money sources available to you, whether it is savings, help from family, or upcoming unemployment compensation. Showing your wife that you have a financial cushion, however small, will help calm her.

▶ Pray with her. This will help both of you feel better.

▶ Remind your wife on a regular basis that it is God who really provides for your family and that He will lead you to another job.

> My God will fully satisfy every need of yours according to his riches in glory in Christ Jesus.
> Philippians 4:19, NRSV

91

How can you help her heal when you've hurt her?

You know the second you have done it. You can see it in her face. That callous thing you said, that thoughtless thing you did, that terrible mistake you can't take back—you have hurt her. If you could take a step back in time you would do things differently, but you are stuck in the present and looking desperately for a way to restore your relationship. What can you do to heal the hurt you caused?

answer

A wound from a thoughtless remark can be quickly stanched by a heartfelt apology and a hug and a kiss. But a bigger offense requires a deeper cleansing and a bigger bandage. If you have done something that has put your relationship in danger, your wife will need more than a simple "I'm sorry." That, of course, is a good place to begin, but be prepared to repeat yourself many times, because once is simply not enough to cover the wound. When you have done something grievous, the first thing you must do is to allow your wife to drain herself of all her hurt and anger. Draining those feelings will require the use of a lot of words, so let her talk. And as she talks, listen penitently, with no defensiveness.

Apologizing is the first step. Change is the second. Your wife needs to see a new-and-improved you, a man who won't hurt her that way again. What you do after you say "I'm sorry" is as important as getting out those tough words, but your behavior will prove to her what is in your heart well beyond what you say. When you live like a changed man, her overtaxed emotions can settle down, and she can start to feel better. And with time she will, because she loves you and she wants things to be better between you. It isn't time that heals all wounds, it is love: yours and hers.

worth thinking about

▶ **Healing is not** always a fast process. Allow your wife as much time as she needs to recover from her hurt.

▶ **The errant husband** bringing home flowers is a cliché, but don't let that stop you from giving her flowers or some other small gift, not as a bribe, but as a symbol of your changed heart and a new beginning.

▶ **Ask what you** can do to make things better. Then be willing to do whatever she needs. This may be humbling, but do it anyway. You would want her to do the same for you if your positions were reversed.

> *A broken spirit, a spirit rightly broken, a heart truly contrite, is to God an excellent thing.*
> John Bunyan

question

▼

How can you comfort her when a family member dies?

You know that nothing is worse than losing someone you love, and when this happens to your wife you find yourself at a loss. What can you say to make things better? What can you do to help her? You can't bring back the one who is gone. You can't even make your wife stop crying. You feel helpless and useless. What can you, as a loving husband, do for her at a time like this?

answer

▼

Death and the loss it brings is the hardest thing a person can face, which makes the grief it leaves in its wake the most difficult of all sorrows to comfort. There is no shortcut out of mourning, but there is comfort. Comfort for your wife comes from your strong arms wrapped around her, from your listening ear and your helpful presence. When someone dies, the ones left behind become doubly precious. Your wife will need lots of holding because she will need physical reassurance that she still has people here who care about her. She will need to talk about the one she lost, about how much that person meant to her, and about how much she will miss that person. She may say things that don't sound rational to you, and she may rant about the unfairness of it all. When she does, don't rush in with theological explanations, wise cautions, or philosophical arguments. Just be there and be sympathetic.

Don't think that it lies entirely with you to step in and fill that gap left by the one who is gone. You can't. You already have your hands full being your wife's husband. God will fill the emptiness in her heart in His own time and His own perfect way. Meanwhile, He expects you to act as His light in a dark time, holding your wife's hand and reassuring her that she is not alone.

worth thinking about

▶ **Coping with death** is all-consuming, and the everyday chores of life look like a complete waste of time. Your wife is probably barely going to want to eat, let alone cook for anyone else. Take up the slack at home, and take over the daily chores.

▶ **Hold your wife** and pray for her. Thank God for the hope of heaven and the good life of the one who has gone before.

▶ **Don't avoid talking** about the one she has lost. She wants to hear the good things about her loved one. It keeps the loved one's memory alive.

> *O, death, where is your victory?*
> *O death, where is your sting?*
> 1 Corinthians 15:55, NLT

question

▼

Why does your wife like to mother you?

Sometimes you wonder if your mother and your wife set up some kind of tag-team arrangement the day you married because your wife often takes over where Mom left off. Why does your wife think she needs to remind you to take along a raincoat when you go outside so you won't catch cold? Why does she behave like the food police, making sure you eat your broccoli and take your vitamins? Why does she sometimes act more like your mother than your wife?

answer

▼

Your wife is hardwired to mother the people she cares about, whether it's you, the kids, or her baby brother. She would never see her behavior as a failure to treat you like a grown-up. She knows you are a grown-up. She simply sees you as a grown-up who needs her help. So if she chases after you with a raincoat, it is because she truly doesn't want you to catch cold. What may seem like light drizzle to you probably looks like a downpour in the making to her, and she doesn't want you to end up cold and miserable or, worse yet, sick. It's just that simple. If you sense a bit of a condescending motherly attitude when she hands over the raincoat, it may be because she simply doesn't get why you make a habit of refusing to take this simple health precaution.

You probably give your colon little consideration. Your wife, however, is fully aware of the dangers of colon cancer, and rather than lose you from that disease, she will morph into your mother to make sure she gets enough roughage into you.

If your wife sees an immediate need in you, she will focus on that rather than on your pride or even on whether or not you want her help. This is because she takes her job of helping you seriously. Even though you find it frustrating, remember that, to her, mothering you is a measure of how much she cares.

worth thinking about

▶ Just as you see it as your job to protect her, she sees it as her job to keep you well. This would explain the scolds you get when you climb onto rickety ladders or take on too much overtime and become exhausted.

▶ Tell your wife when she is mothering you too much and explain that it makes you feel like a boy rather than a man.

▶ When she's mothering you on small issues, go along with it. Broccoli really is good for you.

> Who can find a virtuous and capable wife? She is more precious than rubies. Her husband can trust her, and she will greatly enrich his life.
> Proverbs 31:10–11, NLT

question

▼

Does she recruit help because she thinks you're not capable?

One day your wife looks at you with love in her eyes. She tells you she thinks you are great. She makes you feel like you are on top of the world. Another day she smiles and gently pushes you off by suggesting she find you some help for that big project. "Let's call Bill." And you wonder, *Why do we need to call Bill? Is this what she really thinks of me, that I am helpless, incapable of figuring this thing out on my own?*

answer

▼

When your wife recruits help for you, she is motivated by many things. When you are about to take on a big job, she wants to lighten your load. When you face a complex challenge, she wants to put extra brainpower at your disposal. When she is worried that you are about to enter uncharted territory, she wants to put someone at your back. The one thing your wife doesn't think of when she recruits help is that she is insulting you. Why would she? In a woman's world, helping each other is almost an everyday occurrence.

When a woman faces a big job, she calls her friends and asks for help. To her this is no sign of weakness. It is simply being sensible. Why struggle on her own when her girlfriends will help her? Women offer to bring food to parties, not because they think the hostess can't cook, but because they want to lighten her load. Women are communal, and working together works for them. So the next time your wife wants to recruit help for you, know that she has your best interests at heart. She's probably thinking of your time, your spine, and the sociability of your good buddies. It isn't that you *need* help. It's more like it would be more fun and more efficient for you. Don't take it as an insult, at least not an intentional one.

worth thinking about

▶ Explain to your wife that you find satisfaction in mastering a project without help. Assure her that you will ask for help when you need it.

▶ Don't be stubborn to prove a point. If you need help, admit it. This doesn't make you less of a man. It shows you know how to work smarter, not harder. You might even find that your wife and her friends are onto something.

▶ Always give your wife's motives the benefit of the doubt. She still thinks you are great.

> *Many hands make light work.*
> John Heywood

question

▼

Why does she have to do three things at once?

You and your wife are talking when, halfway through the conversation, she says something to one of the kids. Obviously, she isn't giving you her full attention if she is carrying on two conversations at once. Did she even hear what you just said? Apparently she did, because she picks up right where you left off, all the while starting some new chore. She can never just sit and relax with you. She's always doing something else besides. What's with that?

answer

▼

Your wife's brain is wired differently from yours. You are focused and single-minded. If you are working on the car you work on the car, and that is it. If you are watching the game on TV, you are watching TV. Period. Your wife, on the other hand, will watch TV while knitting a sweater or even reading a book. Or she will watch her favorite show while talking to her sister on the phone. Sis never doubts for a minute that she is being heard. In fact, she is probably doing two things at once also. Women are huge multitaskers. They have to be. A woman doesn't always have the luxury of cooking a meal in peace, not with a toddler hanging on her leg or a baby on her hip. She often has to field PTO phone calls while helping grade-schoolers with their homework. Her mind works the way she talks, with thoughts going several different directions at once.

And she likes it that way. Being able to track more than one thing comes in handy when she has so much she needs to get done. You are still number one in your wife's book—her favorite page, in fact—so don't worry that you have lost her attention when she goes into multitask mode. She's just doing what she has been wired to do.

worth thinking about

▶ **If your wife** is conversing with both the kids and you at the same time, it may be because she is short on time and long on chores, errands, and people to help. Pitch in and lighten her load, and you may find it easier to get her undivided attention.

▶ **When you do** need her undivided attention, ask her for a moment alone and lead her to a quiet corner of the house where you can converse uninterrupted.

▶ **Take her away** from the temptation to multitask by taking a walk or going out for coffee.

> *A woman's work is never done.*
> Sixteenth-century English Proverb

Why are men and women so different?

God is the one who has made us different as male and female. God is the one who brings us together with the idea that we will complete one another.

Bob Lepine

96

question

What does your wife see in Dr. Phil?

You know about Dr. Phil and all those other talk-show hosts who bring people onto their shows to air their problems for the whole world to see. That is just plain scary. And even scarier is the fact that your wife never misses an opportunity to watch the guy. Sometimes she even quotes him. "How's that working for ya?" Frankly, the good doctor doesn't work for you at all. What does she see in him, anyway?

answer

You can sum up why your wife enjoys listening to people like Dr. Phil in two words: *improving relationships*. Because people are important to her, she is fascinated by anything having to do with relationships. And she is always looking for ways to improve hers—with you, with her family, with her friends. She watches a show like *Dr. Phil* and gleans suggestions she can apply to her own life. "Oh, my! Is that what my husband thinks when I act like that? Maybe I need to make some changes." She may find some great self-help tip for her best friend. "Janice, turn on Dr. Phil. He's talking about women who have problems with their mother-in-laws." You see no reason to look to a perfect stranger to help you solve your problems. But this is the woman who likes to recruit help for you at every turn, so it should hardly be surprising that she tunes in to the big bald guy with the folksy sayings. Dr. Phil is the king of help.

Don't worry that your wife has developed some sick obsession with other people's problems. She hasn't. Let her enjoy her daily dose of pop psychology. You never know. She may actually pick up some good tips for handling sticky situations. There may come a day when something she's learned comes in handy and you find yourself glad she enjoys listening to those self-help gurus.

worth thinking about

▶ **If you find her** reading something by Dr. Phil or a book by some well-known marriage expert, that doesn't mean your wife has stopped loving you. She is simply looking for ways to make things even better between you.

▶ **Don't make fun** of her viewing choice. She's gathering expert advice and learning, the same as you do when you watch programs on money management or home improvement.

▶ **Keep the kids** distracted so she can watch the show in peace. That sort of kind gesture is what keeps a marriage healthy and a husband safe from finding himself on the *Dr. Phil* show.

> *What do men and women talk about? Men talk about sports, money, and business. Women often discuss people, feelings, and relationships.*
> Judith Tingley

97 question
Why isn't your wife into gadgets the way you are?

Your wife gets excited about things like scented candles, but she doesn't get revved up over that cool automatic deicer for the car or the fabulous power tool that does everything but fetch you a cool drink when you are working. Gadgets are great. Your wife doesn't get into them the way you do, though, even when they can make running the house so much more fun. After all, what's not to love about a riding lawn mower? Where is her gadget appreciation gene?

answer

Your wife does have a gadget appreciation gene. It just happens to be smaller than yours. But if you'll look around your kitchen, you may see evidence of it in the form of high-tech baking tools or those cute little decorative cheese spreaders. She does like things that make her life easier. She likes to have an up-to-date vacuum, and she enjoys that iPod now that she has figured out how to work it. But she probably doesn't drool over the latest in stereo speakers, and chances are if someone in your home is lobbying for a flat-panel, high-definition TV, it is you and not her. That is because gadgets are so . . . mechanical. And technical. They require a knowledge of a whole different language that few women understand. And who has the time to sit for hours and figure out how to work those new gadgets? She doesn't. Anyway, if she is going to devote hours to something, chances are it will be scrapbooking or shopping or something equally female-friendly.

It all comes down to wiring and preferences. When you were taking apart the family phone and trying to reassemble it, she was probably playing with her friends or reading a book. She is probably happy when you find a special new tool or amazing bit of technology, but if her eyes don't light up at the sight of it, don't worry. It's simply a case of different wiring, different tools.

worth thinking about

▶ **If you are hoping** for a special gadget for Christmas, give your wife all the necessary details so she can find it. Remember, she feels just as lost in an electronics or auto-supply store as you do in a lingerie shop.

▶ **Sometimes women** avoid gadgets because they look too complicated to use. If you buy your wife something you think she will enjoy, make sure you take time to help her master using it.

▶ **If you are** debating between getting your wife that cool new kitchen gadget or some perfume, let the perfume win the debate.

> *From the perspective of a non gadget lover*
> *a new gadget is like getting homework.*
> Bill Adler Jr.

question

▼

What are the pluses of that long memory of hers?

You've heard the old saying that elephants never forget, but when it comes to remembering, you are convinced that no elephant on the planet can match your wife in memory skills. She remembers everything: anniversaries (even the anniversary of your first date), the times you have forgotten anniversaries, every dumb thing you have ever said or done as a husband. Sometimes you wish she didn't have such a good memory. Are there ways that long memory of hers works in your favor?

answer

▼

When it is not working in your favor, you hate the fact that your wife has such a long memory. You find yourself wishing she had a faulty memory chip. Why can't she erase that time you forgot about your date from her memory banks? She can't because her mind holds on to all things emotional. Whatever the experience, if she has an emotional reaction tied to it, she won't easily forget it. This, however, can be good news for you. It means that she won't just remember the times you messed up. She will also remember all the things you did right, like that time six years ago when you saw her all dolled up for New Year's Eve and told her how fabulous she looked.

Within a week you will forget about the flower you picked for her on the way home from work. She will remember it for years.

Every good thing you say and do gets tucked away in her mind to be brought out later and savored. This is how she gets through the hard times. This is how she keeps on loving you even when you aren't being lovable. Her memory is her best tool for coping. And her memory is your best friend because it is what she uses to preserve your kind words and loving gestures in her heart. And when she needs to, she will look down that long memory of hers, and see the man she loves: you at your best.

worth thinking about

▶ **Take advantage** of her gift of memory by enlisting her help in keeping track of important birthdays and anniversaries, especially your wedding anniversary.

▶ **Remember that** what you say and do now will be filed away in her heart, so give her plenty of good memories to store.

▶ **When the two** of you are facing a hard time or a difficult challenge, ask your wife to recall out loud some of the good things you have experienced together in the past. This will encourage you both and keep you going. Good memories really are a gift.

> *God gave us our memories so that we might have roses in winter.*
> Sir James Matthew Barrie

question

99

Why does she take so long to get to the point?

Whether it is big news or simply an update on what happened that day, you want to hear what your wife has to say. Your only wish sometimes is that she would say it a little more quickly. The journey from her first word to the point of the story can become a winding road with many side trips, and you find yourself getting lost. *Where are we going with this?* you wonder. *Why can't we take the conversational freeway?*

answer

Your wife views conversation much as she views travel, which means that when she is telling you something, the details on the way to the end of her story are as important as the end itself. Why rush to the point when there are so many important things to tell along the way? She wants you to have the full experience, to know everything that led up to what she wants to tell you about. After all, if you don't see the whole picture, how can you know what to think? And anyway, the story is interesting. Why wouldn't you want all the fascinating details?

When your wife tells you something, she is not only laying out the facts, she is also helping you see the nuances behind the facts. She wants you to know what happened, what could have happened, and what should have happened. She also wants to tell you how she felt because she knows her feelings are important to you. That all takes time, and if she is recounting something to a friend, she might take even longer because to rush to the point would be brusque and would make the listener feel as if she didn't care enough to take the time for a thorough explanation. So next time your wife starts talking, remember that she has a destination and will not only make sure you get there, she'll also make sure you pick up all the information you need along the way.

worth thinking about

▶ You may want to listen in a hurry, but if your wife has chosen the conversational scenic route, you have to slow down your internal idle.

▶ When you feel that you are getting confused, ask for clarification.

▶ Even when you feel frustrated waiting for your wife to get to the point, remember your manners. Remarks like "Is there a point to this?" will irritate her or hurt her feelings, and you don't want to do either. If you feel you won't have the patience to follow her, politely ask for the *Reader's Digest* version before she begins to relate her story.

> The goal in gender communication is not to change the style of communication but to adapt to the differences.
> Rhonda H. Kelley

question

How do your differences complement each other?

Do you ever find yourself wondering if your wife is not just a different gender but a different species entirely? Her thought processes are nothing like yours, and while she feels the same emotions, she certainly expresses them differently. Many of the things that thrill her leave you mystified. So do the things that anger her. And yet you were both made to complement each other. What are some of the best ways you do that?

answer

Your differences complement each other much the way contrasting colors bring a painting to life. Alone, one of you reflects the image of God quite nicely. Together, though, the two of you show even more facets of God's image and show off His incredible creativity. Together you display hard and soft, strong and gentle, fierce and sweet. Your force is directed by her caution, your anger by her mercy. Her physical weakness is balanced by your strength, and her insight and mercy can save you from the lack of caution that can ride on the back of anger. One of you is practical, and the other is more free-spirited, and that keeps fun in your life and at the same time gives you control and order. One of you likes to clown around, and one of you likes to laugh. One of you likes to cry, and the other likes to comfort. One of you wants to touch, and the other loves to be touched.

Your life journey together as husband and wife will always be filled with contradictions and differences. And just when you think you have finally figured out your wife, she will do something to mystify you. The differences and the never-ending mystery are part of what keeps your marriage interesting. As different as you both are, you fit together beautifully every time you hold each other. And as different as you are, your hearts were designed by God to beat as one.

worth thinking about

▶ **Your differences** combined make the two of you more together than you ever were alone.

▶ **Thank God** for the fact that your wife is different from you. Those differences keep you thinking and on your toes and make life fun and exciting.

▶ **You and your wife** will never think exactly alike. You will always see the world through different eyes. But that is okay as long as you both are looking to God for guidance.

> *God made male and female equal,*
> *he also made them different.*
> John R. W. Stott

Readers who enjoyed this
book will also enjoy

100 Answers to 100 Questions About God

100 Answers to 100 Questions About God's Promises

100 Answers to 100 Questions About Loving Your Husband

100 Answers to 100 Questions About Prayer

100 Answers to 100 Questions to Ask Before You Say "I Do"